T0294466

KING DOHA
Saraha's Advice to a King

Books by Traleg Kyabgon

Integral Buddhism: Developing All Aspects of One's Personhood, Shogam Publications, 2018

Letter to a Frienda: Nagarjuna's Classic Text, Shogam Publications, 2018

Song of Karmapa: The Aspiration of the Mahamudra of True Meaning by Lord Rangjung Dorje, Shogam Publications, 2018

Moonbeams of Mahamudra: The Classic Meditation Manual, Shogam Publications, 2015

Karma: What it is, What it isn't, and Why it matters, Shambhala Publications, 2015

Four Dharmas of Gampopa, KTD Publications, 2013

Asanga's Abhidharmasamuccaya, KTD Publications, 2013

Ninth Karmapa Wangchuk Dorje's Ocean Of Certainty, KTD Publications, 2011

Influence of Yogacara on Mahamudra, KTD Publications, 2010

The Practice of Lojong: Cultivating Compassion through Training the Mind, Shambhala Publications, 2007

Mind at Ease: Self-Liberation through Mahamudra Meditation, Shambhala Publications, 2004

Benevolent Mind: A Manual in Mind Training, Zhyisil Chokyi Ghatsal Publications, 2003

The Essence of Buddhism: An Introduction to Its Philosophy and Practice, Shambhala Publications, 2002 & 2014

Photo facing page: Traleg Kyabgon Rinpoche the Ninth

KING DOHA
Saraha's Advice to a King

Translation and Oral Commentary
Traleg Kyabgon

Foreword by Orgyen Chowang Rinpoche

SHOGAM
PUBLICATIONS
2018

Shogam Publications Pty Ltd
PO Box 239 Ballarat, Victoria, Australia, 3353
www.shogam.org
info@shogam.com

Printed in Australia and the United States of America

Edited by Lynette Hutchison
Designed by David Bennett

National Library of Australia
Kyabgon, Traleg, 1955
King Doha: Saraha's Advice to a King

Printed book ISBN: 978-0-6481148-6-4 (paperback)
E-book ISBN: 978-0-6481148-7-1

DEDICATION

To the fulfillment of the aspirations of
Traleg Kyabgon IXth and all those who
manifest wisdom mind.

Contents

Foreword

I had the good fortune to meet Traleg Rinpoche in 2009 when he was visiting the San Francisco Bay Area with our mutual friend Sam Bercholz. We had a very engaging and celebratory dinner the first night we met and proceeded to become very good friends over the next few years.

The more I got to know Traleg Rinpoche the more I realized what a special and unique master he was. Traleg Rinpoche had a truly deep and profound understanding of the enlightened wisdom of the Buddha as embodied in the Kagyü and Nyingma traditions. One of Traleg Rinpoche's many unique and special qualities was that he was able to skillfully combine his deep passion and understanding of western philosophy and psychology within his presentation of the Buddhadharma. As a result Traleg Rinpoche was able to present the timeless wisdom of the Buddha's teachings in a very modern and contemporary manner in order to benefit students all over the world.

Another special quality of Traleg Rinpoche's was that he was fearless and often presented the teachings of the Buddha in a very unconventional manner. Traleg Rinpoche's extraordinary and deep understanding of the Buddha's teachings allowed him to live and teach in a very creative and vibrant way.

This book is a great reminder of what a special teacher Traleg Rinpoche was as readers will be very inspired by his commentary on the great master Saraha's text *King Doha* on the ground, path and fruition of Mahamudra. By reading and contemplating the teachings found in this beautiful commentary you will also receive a taste of Traleg Rinpoche's extraordinary realization.

Orgyen Chowang Rinpoche
Author of Our Pristine Mind
Founder & Spiritual Director of
Pristine Mind Foundation
San Francisco Bay Area
25th May 2018

Biography of Author
TRALEG KYABGON RINPOCHE IX

Traleg Kyabgon Rinpoche IX (1955-2012) was born in Nangchen in Kham, eastern Tibet. He was recognized by His Holiness XVI Gyalwang Karmapa as the ninth Traleg tulku and enthroned at the age of two as the supreme abbot of Thrangu Monastery. Rinpoche was taken to Rumtek Monastery in Sikkim at the age of four where he was educated with other young tulkus in exile by His Holiness Karmapa for the next five years.

Rinpoche began his studies under the auspices of His Eminence Kyabje Thuksey Rinpoche at Sangngak Choling in Darjeeling. He also studied with a number of other eminent Tibetan teachers during that time and mastered the many Tibetan teachings with the Kagyü and Nyingma traditions in particular including the *Hevajra Tantra*, *Guhyasamaja Tantra*, and the third Karmapa's *Zabmo Nangdon* (*The Profound Inner Meaning*) under Khenpo Noryang (abbot of Sangngak Choling). Rinpoche studied the *Abhidharmakosha*, *Pramanavarttika*, *Bodhisattvacharyavatara*, *Abhidharmasamuccaya*, *Six Treaties of Nagarjuna*, the *Madhyantavibhaga*, and the *Mahayanuttaratantra* with Khenpo Sogyal. He also studied with Khenpo Sodar and was trained in tantric ritual practices by Lama Ganga, who had been specifically sent by His Holiness Karmapa for that purpose.

In 1967 Rinpoche moved to the Institute of Higher Tibetan Studies in Sarnath, and studied extensively for the next five years.

He studied Buddhist history, Sanskrit, and Hindi, as well as Longchenpa's *Finding Comfort and Ease* (*Ngalso Korsum*), *Seven Treasuries* (*Longchen Dzod Dun*), *Three Cycles of Liberation* (*Rangdrol Korsum*), and *Longchen Nyingthig* with Khenchen Palden Sherab Rinpoche and Khenpo Tsondru.

When Rinpoche had completed these studies at the age of sixteen, he was sent by His Holiness Karmapa to study under the auspices of the Venerable Khenpo Yeshe Chodar at Sanskrit University in Varanasi for three years. Rinpoche was also tutored by khenpos and geshes from all four traditions of Tibetan Buddhism during this time.

Rinpoche was subsequently put in charge of Zangdog Palri Monastery (the glorious copper colored mountain) in Eastern Bhutan and placed under the private tutelage of Dregung Khenpo Ngedon by His Holiness Karmapa to continue his studies of Sutra and Tantra. He ran this monastery for the next three years and began learning English during this time.

From 1977 to 1980, Rinpoche returned to Rumtek in Sikkim to fill the honored position of His Holiness' translator, where he dealt with many English-speaking Western visitors.

Rinpoche moved to Melbourne, Australia in 1980 and commenced studies in religion and philosophy at LaTrobe University. Rinpoche established E-Vam Institute in Melbourne in 1982 and went on to establish further Centers in Australia, America and New Zealand. For the next 25 years Rinpoche gave weekly teachings, intensive weekend courses, and retreats on classic Kagyu and Nyingma texts. During this time Rinpoche also taught internationally travelling extensively through America, Europe, and South East Asia and was appointed the Spiritual Director of Kamalashila Institute in Germany for five years in the 1980's.

Rinpoche established a retreat center, Maitripa Centre in Healesville, Australia in 1997 where he conducted two public retreats a year. Rinpoche founded E-Vam Buddhist Institute in the US in 2000, and Nyima Tashi Buddhist Centre in New Zealand 2004. In 2010 Rinpoche established a Buddhist college called Shogam Vidhalaya at E-Vam Institute in Australia and instructed students on a weekly basis.

Throughout his life Rinpoche gave extensive teachings on many aspects of Buddhist psychology and philosophy, as well as comparative religion, and Buddhist and Western thought. He was an active writer and has many titles to his name. Titles include: the best selling *Essence of Buddhism*; *Karma, What It Is, What It Isn't, and Why It Matters*; *The Practice of Lojong*; *Moonbeams of Mahamudra*; and many more. Many of Rinpoche's books are translated in to a number of different languages including Chinese, French, German, Korean and Spanish. Rinpoche's writings are thought provoking, challenging, profound, and highly relevant to today's world and its many challenges.

Rinpoche was active in publishing during the last two decades of his life, beginning with his quarterly magazine *Ordinary Mind* which ran from 1997 to 2003. Further, Rinpoche founded his own publishing arm Shogam Publications in 2008 and released a number of books on Buddhist history, philosophy, and psychology and left instructions for the continuation of this vision. His vision for Shogam and list of titles can be found at www.shogam.com.

Rinpoche's ecumenical approach can be seen in his other activities aimed at bringing buddhadharma to the West. He established the biannual Buddhism and Psychotherapy Conference (1994 - 2003), and Tibet Here and Now Conference (2005), and the annual Buddhist Summer School (1984 to the present).

Traleg Kyabgon Rinpoche IX passed into parinirvana on 24 July 2012, on Chokhor Duchen, the auspicious day of the Buddha's first teaching. Rinpoche stayed in meditation (*thugdam*) for weeks after his passing. A traditional cremation ceremony was conducted at

Maitripa Centre and a stupa was erected on the center's grounds in Rinpoche's honor.

It is a privilege to continue to release the profound teachings of Traleg Kyabgon Rinpoche IX given in the West for over 30 years. Rinpoche's Sangha hope that many will benefit.

Acknowledgements

Taking oral teachings through to publication is rarely the work of one individual; it includes all those who assisted Traleg Rinpoche IXth in various ways throughout his teaching career. In particular, however, I would like to thank Carolyn MacLennan and Valda Hutchison for transcribing the talks; Kathleen Gregory, Gabriel Lafitte, Hugh Williams, and Cathy Wylie for their editorial support; Claire Blaxell, David Bennett and Salvatore Celiento for their attention to detail; and Felicity Lodro, without whom the project would have remained entirely theoretical.

Lynette Hutchison

Editor's Introduction

Traleg Kyabgon Rinpoche IXth (1955-2012) was a contemporary Tibetan Buddhist teacher well versed in the traditional texts not only of his own lineage, the Kagyu school of Tibetan Buddhism, but of Tibetan Buddhism in general. Throughout his life he showed a keen interest and aptitude for scholarship and extended this to his personal studies of Western philosophy, psychology, culture and theology. He was an avid reader and fluent in English. His reason for mastering English was to obviate the need for a translator: this was his gift to the West. He gave oral teachings in a variety of formats ranging from overviews of Buddhist perspectives to commentaries on key texts, always taking care to ensure the author's intended meaning of any text he taught was his main focus. The range and immediacy which characterized Rinpoche's teachings provided some challenges in bringing the material for this book together. In sharing those challenges, I hope that readers will gain a deeper appreciation of the task Traleg Rinpoche IXth undertook when he chose to spend his life bringing the Dharma to the West.

The material presented in this book was taken from two separate sets of oral teachings: an overview of Mahamudra taught at Karma Triyana Dhamachakra, USA, 2009; and the commentary to Saraha's *King Doha* taught at Evam USA in upstate New York in 2003. The overview offers the reader a thorough introduction to Mahamudra, as well as an understanding of how the Mahamudra approach sits in relation to other approaches found with Buddhism.

As an introduction to the commentary on Saraha's verses, the *Overview of Mahamudra* serves two purposes. Firstly, it provides the conceptual context necessary to appreciate the intent of Saraha's work. For example, the notion of fixation and the many forms it can take is discussed at length. This culminates in an examination of the ways in which a practitioner can stray with their practice. In doing so it acts as a fitting springboard to launch into the commentary on the King Doha.

Secondly, it introduces many terms found in Mahamudra literature, and these terms have their origins in the approaches of such practitioners as Saraha, whom Traleg Rinpoche credits with being the forefather of the Mahamudra tradition. It is often the case that the same term in Tibetan has been translated into English in several different ways by different translators. This is sometimes necessary as a particular term can have one meaning when used in a sutric context but another when used by, for example, a Dzogchenpa. In many cases though, there is no exact English equivalent for the term and a variety of options have been selected as a "best fit" by translators. The Overview of Mahamudra then introduces the reader to many of the Tibetan or Sanskrit terms relevant to the Saraha commentary along with Traleg Rinpoche's explanations of their meanings.

The *King Doha*[1] refers to a set of 40 root verses traditionally grouped with two other of Saraha's dohas, commonly known as the *People Doha* and the *Queen Doha*. There are a number of existent translations of the root verses, as well as commentary texts. When it comes to this part of the book, Traleg Rinpoche does not enter into any discussion of the authenticity of the *King Doha* as a work by Saraha, but instead focuses on helping us understand its message to the practitioner. For the commentary to the 40 root verses, Traleg Rinpoche relies on the work of the Tibetan commentator, Karma Trinlépa,[2] whose 16th Century work is respected within the Kagyu tradition. Karma Trinlépa's commentary[3] contains commentaries on all three of Saraha's dohas mentioned. The dohas themselves, and in particular the *King Doha*, being elliptical and evocative poetry, are not easy to understand without considerable background in Tibetan approaches to meditation. Accessing them through the works of a commentator is a traditional way to study them.

This is not the first time Karma Trinlépa's commentary has been presented in English. Herbert Guenther translated it in *The Royal Song of Saraha*,[4] first published in 1969, and used it, along with another commentary on the same text by Kyemé Dechen,[5] to inform his translation of the 40 root verses of the King Doha. This was a remarkable undertaking and Traleg Rinpoche expressed respect for Herbert Guenther's work when delivering the talks.

In 2006, in a publication edited by the translator Michele Martin, Khenchen Thrangu Rinpoche's commentary also became available. It is hoped that readers of Traleg Rinpoche's approach to the commentary will also study Khenchen Thrangu Rinpoche's excellent material. There are differences between this work and that of Traleg Rinpoche. To understand this, it is helpful to consider how Tibetan Buddhist teachers traditionally take the background of their audience into account when they teach. In doing so, they are providing a meaning translation rather than a word by word rendition into English. This can result in different points being expanded upon, or even sections being left out for varying reasons.

It should be noted that since *A Song for the King* was not published until 2006, Traleg Rinpoche would not have been in a position to have read Thrangu Rinpoche's commentary prior to the delivery of his 2003 teachings on the *King Doha*. It is clear from the audio recordings of the original talks, however, that during these talks he was provided with what was presumably a draft translation of the root verses by Michele Martin.

In general, it was not Traleg Rinpoche's habit to provide translations of root verses when teaching commentarial material; he usually selected a translation published in English to work from. In the case of the *King Doha*, he directed students to the translations by both Michele Martin and Herbert Guenther. From an editor's point of view, this presented a dilemma. To present the commentary without the root verses was not considered as an option as the reader would have had no basis to appreciate the commentary. As Traleg Rinpoche rarely used the same wording in his commentary as found in either of the translations of the root verses mentioned, a decision was made to retranslate the root verses based on his commentary. Obviously then this version is heavily dependent upon Traleg Rinpoche's translation of Karma Trinlépa's interpretation. Also, as this translation of the root verses was neither done by Traleg Rinpoche himself nor authorized by him, readers should be very careful to focus primarily on the commentary.

Why study Saraha?

One of the reasons Saraha requires such careful study is that he uses a system to describe the progressive stages of realization through Mahamudra practice not found in later works on Mahamudra such as Takpo Tashi Namgyal's *Moonbeams of Mahamudra*. There is little material is available in English to explain this system, though Michele Martin's introduction to *A Song for the King* addresses this lack and links it to the more commonly described four yogas of Mahamudra.[6] Saraha's system relies on a series of "states," to use Traleg Rinpoche's translation, for the term *da*[7] in Tibetan, which is commonly glossed as "signs." These are: *drenpa, drenmé, kyemé,* and *lodé,*[8] which Traleg Rinpoche translates as "remembrance," "non-remembrance," "uncreated-ness," and "beyond conception."

The overview of Mahamudra that forms the introductory

material does not mention the four states described by Saraha at all, though it does briefly discuss the four yogas under the sub-heading *The four stages of realization in Mahamudra*. In fact, in 30 years of teaching in the West, the teachings that comprise the commentary to Saraha's *King Doha* are the only time Traleg Rinpoche mentions Saraha's specific system, though his terms *drenpa* and *drenmé* are at times referenced. It is in the descriptions found in *The insights of vipashyana* that one starts to see the connections, though these are themselves intimately related to the four stages of realization. Working with Saraha's approach challenges one to delve into Mahamudra manuals more deeply with both study and practice, to appreciate the significance of what is being presented fully. As more English translations of Saraha's other works appear, it is hoped Traleg Rinpoche's commentary will assist in understanding the meaning of these.

As students of Traleg Rinpoche IXth, the Editors of Shogam Publications aim to make available those teachings left behind by Traleg Rinpoche as a guide for practice. The material has been presented to the best of our ability; any errors or omissions are the responsibility of the Editor. We pray that once he has completed his training, the Traleg Yangsi will provide the corrections and answers to questions that it was too late to request from Traleg Rinpoche IXth himself.

Lynette Hutchison

Editor's Biography

Lynette Hutchison first developed an interest in Buddhism whilst travelling in Asia in the early 1980's. She met Traleg Kyabgon Rinpoche IX at the first Buddhist Summer School run by his Buddhist Centre in Melbourne, Australia, in 1984 and remained his student until he passed away in 2012. Having completed a traditional Tibetan three year retreat program under the guidance of Traleg Rinpoche, she continues to explore Buddhism through study and practice.

Introductory Remarks

Saraha is usually credited with the founding of the Mahamudra[9] system of meditation. As such, he holds a very special place in the Kagyü lineage. He was called "Saraha" because of his association with a woman who came from a lower-class background and whose family's profession was that of making arrows. He is thus often depicted with an arrow. Both in his personal life and in terms of his spiritual development, he is considered to have been able to go beyond fixation on such binary notions as high class versus low class and sacred versus profane. In other words, he attained the realization of non-dual wisdom.

Saraha is also regarded as one of the most important of the tantric *mahasiddhas*[10] (Skt.) of India, who despite the reference to tantra in the name, were often teaching something very different from what we would normally regard as Tantrism. They were teaching the approach which came to be known as Mahamudra style meditation. This style of meditation did not involve all the basic ingredients of traditional Tantra practice such as the recitation of mantras, carrying out of rituals, and invocation of deities.

Along with other mahasiddhas, Saraha made the claim that the view of Tantrism is limited and that real practice lies in meditation in the style of Mahamudra, unencumbered by all the ritual and associated paraphernalia of Tantra. This will become clearer when we come to discuss Saraha's advice itself. Before we do so, however, it will be helpful for readers to have some understanding of the

Mahamudra approach. The Mahamudra approach as presented in the overview that follows is taken from the Mahamudra literature that developed after Saraha's passing. As a result, there is some variation in terminology from that used by Saraha in the work we will be considered more closely, the *King Doha*. What is of importance, however, is gaining an appreciation of what the Mahamudra approach is about. With that, Saraha's terminology becomes easier to understand.

OVERVIEW OF MAHAMUDRA

Buddhism:
More than One Approach

Sometimes people think of Mahamudra practice as too esoteric and profound to be practiced by those who are not experienced meditators. From my point of view, though, that's not the right attitude to take. As a practice, Mahamudra is presented gradually. The traditional manuals even teach us how to settle the mind through *shamatha* (Skt.).[11] This in itself implies the intended recipients are not particularly advanced. If they were, one would hope this would be something they would already be familiar with.

Mahamudra teachings are designed for all of us who want to learn something about ourselves and how to deal with our experiences. They are about learning how to *be*, in fact, which is what Mahamudra puts emphasis on. Mahamudra meditation is like other forms of meditation insofar as it teaches how to settle the mind, but Mahamudra teachings, and Dzogchen teachings, for that matter, are quite unique.

They are unique in that they teach us to settle the mind in terms of *how to be*, as opposed to *what to do*. A lot of Buddhist teaching is about what to do and what not to do—you do this, you don't do that, you refrain from this, you engage in that—and if you do this, you will become holy, you will be doing something that other people are not doing. In many ways Buddhism has always taught people to go against the grain. The whole notion of going against samsara is like that. Everybody is immersed in samsara, so anyone who dares to go against samsara is going against the grain, against the mainstream, against what is acceptable and regarded as worth pursuing by most people.

When Buddhism says we become holy through the cultivation of certain virtues, even that is a form of rebellion. It involves non-acceptance of what is normally regarded as the good thing to do. In Mahamudra though, notions of what to accept and what to reject, what to cultivate and what not to cultivate are not encouraged as much. Mahamudra and Dzogchen[12] teachings are not simply about what to do or not do, but, as mentioned earlier, about learning how to *be*.

Generally in Buddhist history, three different kinds of techniques are mentioned in terms of what we should do: renunciation, purification, and transformation. Then there is self-liberation. Self-liberation teaches us how to be—in ourselves, with ourselves—and how to be friendly with the whole gamut of our experiences. Even if an experience is disturbing, we just try to be friendly with it. We try to be with it rather than thinking, "I have to do something, I have to renounce this" or "I have to purify it" or "I have to transform it."

Renunciation

With the idea of renunciation, Buddhism teaches us to renounce bad thoughts, bad emotions, bad attitudes, and bad habits and replace them with good thoughts, good emotions, and good habits. We renounce, we give up and, in order to do that, Buddhism even teaches us to avoid circumstances and situations that may give rise to bad thoughts, bad emotions, and bad feelings. This is why some people become celibate or go into retreat. It is thought that by removing yourself from situations that give rise to strong emotions, you could feel better and give yourself the opportunity to understand how you become entrapped in delusory, samsaric states and how delusory, samsaric experiences are perpetuated.

Purification

Renunciation is one technique we can practice and there is no doubt that it can work. Then there is the technique of purification. This approach suggests, for example, that we don't really have to try to avoid everything we desire. Instead, we look at the nature of the things we desire and, in doing so, purify them. We see that it is not just the things themselves that draw us in but, rather, it is our belief that the things we desire have some kind of intrinsic reality that is the issue.

We tend to think that if we possess this or that thing, we are going to "be somebody" or that as a person we are going to be enriched. Conversely, by not having them, we tend to think we are less of a person. Realizing that whatever we desire has no intrinsic reality in itself releases us from that obsession. Then if we have what we desire it's great, but if we don't, that's okay too. Instead of thinking, "I should not desire these things, I shouldn't have them; the less desire I have the better I will become as a person," one thinks, "even if I have these things, as long as I realize they are just things and do not have any intrinsic worth, that is okay." In other words, they have what in Buddhism is called "relative worth." We see that, relatively speaking, some things are worth more than others but they do not possess the intrinsic worth we attribute to them. That is called purification. We understand these things are in themselves *shunya*[13] (Skt.) or empty. A particular thing is worth something or other based on other things, not because of anything intrinsic to it.

Even though this may seem a simple idea, it is not. Purification, in this sense, means purified by the understanding of *shunyata*[14] (Skt.) or emptiness. If you think carefully about it, this really is very profound. It's as if our mind is designed to latch onto things and say, "this is real," but whatever we attribute to any particular thing or situation or event is just that, an attribution. Nothing in itself has any worth. This is so in terms of what we are doing, what we are trying to achieve, and also what we possess, what we are trying to accumulate.

To give an example, inflation shows very clearly that our money has no intrinsic worth because inflation and deflation dictate its value. Even without Buddhist education, we know money doesn't have intrinsic worth; it is only worth whatever it is worth depending upon context, depending upon other considerations. The notion we are discussing is the same. "Purification" means we understand that.

Then, as Mahayana Buddhism tells us, we can actually dance with life a little more. Even in terms of money, we may in fact become more skillful at handling it because we are not so obsessed with its intrinsic reality. We develop a flexible way of looking at things, and being fluid in terms of how we work with things is always a good thing.

Transformation

The next approach, transformation, is practiced in Tantrism. Tantrism is the Buddhist form of esotericism. Transformation is not only about seeing things in terms of relationships and interdependence, but also seeing how something that may appear really bad or repulsive or disgusting can be turned into something positive, something good, something helpful. For example, in Tantrism we try to transform what we call the five poisons into five wisdoms. So, excessive desire, anger, jealousy, pride, and ignorance can be transformed into discriminating wisdom, mirror-like wisdom, wisdom of accomplishment, wisdom of equanimity, and wisdom of the natural state. The five poisons are transformed into five wisdoms because it is not by renunciation or purification but through transformation that we attain our true selfhood.

Whether you believe it or not, in Buddhism we actually try to attain our own true selfhood. Many people tend to think Buddhism teaches selflessness, so it follows that as Buddhists we are trying to become nothing, nobody, a form of self-extinction. That is a total misunderstanding of what Buddhism is teaching. The notion of self-transformation is emphasized precisely because of that. If there were no "self" to transform, why would we bother? Who would there be to be transformed? Even the notions of renunciation and purification wouldn't make any sense if we really believed there was nobody home. We are trying to really find ourselves and we want to achieve liberation, as we say in Buddhism. We want to find freedom.

Freedom is valued only because there is somebody who is going to benefit from achieving that freedom. If there is nobody who will achieve anything from being free, then what is the point in aiming towards freedom? It would be better to be in bondage than to be free. We seek freedom because we think that if we achieve freedom, liberation, nirvana, then we will be in a different state to what we are in now, that's the key.

Self-transformation also emphasizes that point, but in a different way from the approach of renunciation or purification. We are not saying, "I don't want to be angry, I don't want to be lustful"; we are saying that through lust, through anger we will transform ourselves. We do that by the use of extreme forms of imaginative exercises. We become angrier than we can even imagine. We become more lustful than we can even imagine ourselves being. We manifest ourselves as a wrathful deity wearing a necklace of severed heads and drinking blood from a skull-cup. I am not exaggerating. Instead of restraining ourselves, we are unleashed and give expression to all of our hidden passions. But it is done in a totally symbolic and imaginative way, so nobody is actually harmed. In other words, we give expression to our hidden passions.

Sometimes, as we know, holding things back and repressing them in fact makes us worse; aggression will still come out, and all our hidden passions will find their way out somehow, have an adverse effect on things, and may even hurt people.

Tantric practices are done in such a manner as to use these unbridled emotions and feelings and galvanize that energy for a purpose, for real transformation. We become a different person and are able to give expression to them without doing any harm; instead, benefit is gained from having given expression to these emotions. That is the secret tantric method. The reason it is called secret is because it is a dangerous method to use. Here we shall be talking about the method of self-liberation which is at least easier to discuss, even though it is very profound.

Self-liberation

In Mahamudra, the approach is called self-liberation, *rangdröl*,[15] in Tibetan. It is not the approach of renunciation, purification, or transformation that we have been talking about. *Rang* means self and *dröl* means liberation, so the simplest translation for *rangdröl* is self-liberation.

What this means is that we should just try to be ourselves in the most fundamental sense. It doesn't mean taking a stance, as some people think it does, along the lines of, "I am just an angry bastard, accept me as I am." That is not the Mahamudra approach. Mahamudra instead refers to having a much more fundamental sense of being in our totality or, in other words, being a total person. If we can be with ourselves, then we can have some experience of self-liberation.

We are always thinking such things as, "I need to do something," or, "I need to achieve something." Even when we do meditation, we think like that. We think things like, "Every time I sit, my mind is all over the place," or, "When I first started meditating, I was a bit better, I found some kind of mental equilibrium, but it didn't last." We may even think, "The more I sit, the more agitated my mind becomes, so my meditation is not working." Even with simple things like that, Mahamudra teachings say it is exactly the kind of thing we should be working with. Just *seeing* that in itself is meditation; we don't actually have to do something to change it.

A lot of emphasis is put on recognizing, seeing. If we recognize or see something happening inside us, we are already meditating. If we don't recognize, if we don't see, we are not meditating. It is not the state of mind or the quality of the experience that determines whether we are in Mahamudra meditation or not, but whether we actually see what is going on so that whatever we experience can be self-liberated. Good experience, bad experience, neutral experience—everything can be self-liberated, and that is the key. If we approach our experience this way, we learn how to bring our state of being and experience together—being and the experience. Otherwise we think of experience and being in a totally separate way.

We think we have to look for experiences and that experience is something outside of our being. We may think that if we find certain experiences, then these might allow us to find our own state of being. What Mahamudra says, however, is that if we allow ourselves to be in our own state of being, our primordial state of experience will arise.

In Mahamudra and Dzogchen teachings we talk about primordial experience and the primordial state of being coming together, prior to any specific experience. I suppose you could say our potential for having all kinds of experiences is the primordial experience. That is the level of experience that we work with in Mahamudra. This is the one experience which gives rise to all experiences but is not confined to any one particular experience. It is unconditioned experience which is, as sometimes stated, all-encompassing. When we have that kind of experience, we do not get all worked up about "our experiences." As is said in the teachings, any experience we have is seen in a very fundamental sense as a good experience; even a bad experience is seen as a good. This doesn't mean in the sense of seeing it as a good experience as opposed to a bad experience, but as something beyond. The Mahamudra experience leads us to having that experience which is beyond thinking, "Oh, this is a really wonderful experience" or "this is a horrible experience." With any experience we have, while recognizing it as a good or a bad one, we still have another experience that we would not normally have. That is called self-liberation.

Practicing Mahamudra does not mean we become totally idiotic. It's not that we end up being unable to judge whether something is good or bad, or pleasant or unpleasant. We also don't start thinking, "Oh, this is so painful, I am so great," in a masochistic way.

We don't stop thinking something is good or something is bad, but we are less fixated, we grasp at these things less. Good experiences are already good, so we don't have to worry about them, but bad experiences also do not render us hapless and hopeless. We don't become obsessive about them, bogged down, or thrown into a deep depression where we despair and feel sorry for ourselves and think we are the worst person on the planet.

How to experience things primordially is a very valuable lesson to learn, and we don't have that normally. Our experiences don't get self-liberated because of fixation or obsession. Obsession and fixation are what bind us, entrap us, and keep us from reaching liberation. This is why even good experiences stop being good. Instead of thinking, "Oh, that was a great thing" and enjoying it, and then using that to further our future experiences and bring more joy and enrichment to our lives, we start thinking, "It didn't last, it disappeared, I'll never have that kind of experience again, what a miserable person I am for letting that go." Our life then gets worse by the minute because of our fixation and grasping.

Primordial experience means not doing that kind of thing. Then any kind of experience we have can be self-liberated. We then say things like: unitive experience of bliss and emptiness, appearance and emptiness, and luminosity and emptiness. With the approach of self-liberation, the whole gamut of our experiences can be primordially experienced through these modes: as appearance and emptiness, as bliss and emptiness, as luminosity and emptiness.

Bliss and emptiness experience, for example, doesn't have to do with having some wonderful experience. One can have a painful experience and still primordially experience it as bliss and emptiness or as appearance and emptiness or as luminosity and emptiness.

Contrasting the path of liberation with the path of method

At times the path of liberation, *drölam*[16] (Tib.), is contrasted with and also paired with another approach called *thaplam*[17] (Tib.), which means the path of method. Mahamudra teaches the path of liberation. The tantric practices of transformation as practiced in the Highest Yoga Tantra are the Six Dharmas Naropa[18] employed and they teach the path of method, transformation. The tantric Six Dharmas of Naropa are illusory body yoga, mystic heat yoga, dream yoga, clear light, the transference of consciousness, and the practice of intermediate stage, the bardo.

In the Highest Yoga Tantra, using the path of method, one can also attain Mahamudra. The aim of Highest Yoga Tantric practice is to realize Mahamudra. The route taken to reach Mahamudra is however different to taking Mahamudra itself as the path to liberation. The difference lies in how one practices shamatha and *vipashyana*[19](Skt.) meditation. In Tantrism, Mahamudra is attained through engaging in tantric yogic practices such as mystic heat yoga. By mixing the male and female life essences and so forth, one attains the realization of mind's own innate luminosity or "clear light," thus leading to the realization of Mahamudra. In this particular context, though, we are speaking about Mahamudra in terms of Mahamudra as path to liberation.

Establishing the View

Even though we speak about a *path* to Mahamudra or liberation, nevertheless the path of self-liberation is not like the paths spoken about in other contexts. The paths spoken of in relation to renunciation, purification, and transformation all involve trying to attain something. One is trying to transform oneself by attaining different kinds of experiences, or one is trying to cultivate certain mental attitudes or bolster certain feelings.

With Mahamudra, the aim of the practice is actually to learn to be "in oneself" rather than trying to attain something. In most of the other practices we are using our ordinary mind in trying to transform ourselves. The term "ordinary mind"[20] here is not being used in the sense often found in Mahamudra literature, but ordinary in the sense of using our mind which thinks, which remembers, which has anxieties, fears, and worries.

Combining paying attention with remembrance

If we take a close look at many practices, including those that help us cultivate mindfulness and lead us to become more attentive and observant, we see that what is going on is that we are paying attention to those things we should pay attention to. Mental imprints are then created that leave indelible marks on the psyche. These exert a great deal of influence on our mind. Even our ability to practice mindfulness itself improves because of the fact that we have made the effort to pay attention to certain things. The imprints created by paying attention to certain things act as reminders in turn.

In other words, we develop the habit of remembering to think about the things we should be thinking about, instead of habitually indulging in superfluous or more harmful thoughts or negative emotions. In Buddhism, mindfulness is associated not only with paying attention to the breath or thoughts or whatever the case may be, but with remembrance.

If we just pay attention to certain things without retaining something else, without training the mind to adopt new habits, for instance, there can be no transformation. This is what is meant when it is said that with these approaches, we are generally trying to manipulate the mind. We are trying to exploit the mind in terms of its resources.

Understanding the mind

In addition, though, we are trying to understand the mind. This is why we study the Abhidharma.[21] We try to identify all the kinds of thoughts and emotions that are listed and see which thoughts and emotions are helpful and which are not. We try to break down the negative emotions like anger, so that instead of thinking it is all just "anger," we question further to determine such things as whether it is hostility, resentment, or just bare aggression. By using meditation to identify the specific thoughts and emotions that arise in our mind, we begin to understand something about our mind. Here, we are using the lists of mental factors and elements found in Abhidharma in order to help us practice mindfulness and then, in that way, we are transforming our mind.

Adopting an uncontrived approach

All these techniques involve some notion of cause and effect. Certain states of mind, certain thoughts, and certain emotions impact on our mind in specific way and with these techniques, we are trying to work out that causal relationship. We are attempting to establish some link between our feelings, thoughts, and emotions, and our bodily state. We notice that when we have disturbing thoughts, they are almost always accompanied by negative feelings, and then negative bodily states, sensations, and so forth. When we are in a state such as aggression, the physical sensations that we feel are also very unpleasant; it is not a pleasant state to be in. We thus make connections, and by making these connections we try to transform ourselves.

In Mahamudra, however, we are not trying to transform our mind. In the language of Mahamudra, all these approaches are called "contrived methods," *chöpa*,[22] in Tibetan. Even meditation approached this way is called *chöpai gom*.[23] The Mahamudra approach to meditation, on the other hand, is called "non-contrived" or the "uncontrived" approach to meditation. Having an uncontrived approach to meditation means one is not trying to create some kind of special state of mind in order to have a meditative experience.

The main aim is to simply try to be "in oneself," the Mahamudra view being that if we allow ourselves to be in our natural state, we will automatically enter into a meditative state. In other words, it is natural for us to be in a meditative state, and it is unnatural not to be in a meditative state.

Learning how to simply be

As being in a meditative state is to be oneself, it is not the case that we have to create a special mental state called the meditative state. If we learn to simply be in ourselves, we will be in our natural state and, being in a natural state, we will be free. Everything that then arises in the form of experiences will become self-liberated. Thus the idea used here is that of self-liberation, rather than liberation by someone else.

We do not try to liberate a thought or emotion that has arisen in the mind, be it good or bad. Instead, by simply allowing the thoughts and emotions to rise and fall, we are automatically in a meditative state. That is the fundamental approach taken here, so therefore a lot of teachings are given around the notion of not thinking of discursive or wayward thoughts in a negative way and not thinking of them as disturbances to our meditation.

For example, the first thing one is instructed to do to practice shamatha meditation according to Mahamudra is to be open to varieties of experiences. One's aim is not necessarily to exercise attention on particular mental content in order to develop certain things in ourselves. Instead, the aim is to have the capacity to be open to varieties of experiences, whether pleasant or unpleasant. In this way the aim is to be open to good and bad thoughts, positive and negative emotions, positive and negative feelings. We aim to be open to all of these.

Whether or not we are in a meditative state is not determined by whether we have thoughts or feelings arising in the mind. Instead, if we are taking notice, if we are aware of these things arising in the mind, then we are already liberated. This is so because of the attitude that we try to cultivate, which is called "developing the view of Mahamudra."

Having confidence that buddha is no other

The reason the view is emphasized so much at the beginning is because we do not have confidence that our mind's nature is no different from that of the Buddha. We do not have confidence that the state of enlightenment is not something to be attained but something to be re-discovered.

What we are doing is trying to be in the unconditioned state of our own being. This, as mentioned earlier, is different from dealing with the mind in terms of its thoughts, emotions, and feelings and trying to see what causes what, how these things are interconnected, and so on.

To establish the view, we are taught that the mind's own nature is unconditioned. To say the mind's own nature is unconditioned means it is unproduced; it has not come about due to causes and conditions. If it has not come about due to causes and conditions, then we cannot bring it about even through practice; it has to be present right from the beginning, as it is traditionally put.

Being in the state of authenticity

This connects with what was mentioned earlier, in terms of primordial experience. This experience of being in the state of authenticity is not something that comes about because of some changing mental state. Instead, it comes from being able to rest in one's own natural state. This is called the uncontrived state, and understanding the view is important because we don't have that realization, we are not buddhas yet.

We do not really have any understanding that our own intrinsic nature is not different from that of the buddhas. We have to have some conceptual understanding of that. To establish that conceptual understanding, we say we have to think of our own intrinsic nature as uncaused, unconditioned, and not produced; that it has not come about due to causes and conditions. If something comes about due to causes and conditions, then what is gained can also be lost, as these teachings say.

Understanding the different aspects of the mind

What we have to understand then is the so-called ordinary mind that we have been talking about. We have to understand the relationship between the mind that thinks, remembers, feels, and so on, and what we call the "nature of the mind." To establish the view, it has to be made very clear that there is a big difference between the nature of the mind and what we know to be the mind.

In order to understand our mind, it is spoken about in relation to its three different aspects. As it is put in Tibetan, *ngowo chik la dokpa thadé*[24] which means "same reality, but conceptually thought of in different ways." Breaking this down, *ngowo chik* means "one reality" and *dokpa thadé* means "conceptually thought of in different ways." We thus speak about the nature of the mind, the essence of the mind, and the characteristic of the mind.

The nature of the mind is uncaused, or unoriginated, which is another term often used in this context, which means it is like open space; mind in itself is unbounded and totally free and spacious. Mind's unbounded nature, though, is not like a vacuum; it is not like a big hole but is luminous. The essence of the mind is said to be luminous. When we say, "try to remain in the natural state," what we mean is that we try to remain in that state of unboundedness, with a sense of luminosity. We can do this even with unceasing thoughts, as the Mahamudra teachings point out. The thoughts, emotions, feelings, and so on that flood the mind—all the activities that are going on in the mind—are called the "characteristic of the mind." The characteristic of the mind does not have to be blocked out, because whatever arises in the form of the characteristic of the mind, arises from the natural state and then dissipates back into the natural state.

Many different images are used for this. For example, one is snow falling down on a rock, where as soon as the snow hits the rock, it scatters and then simply settles on the ground. Similarly when we have discursive thoughts arising, they arise and then they dissipate. In other words, we do not have to try to make them go away.

Appreciating what meditation is about

The mind's own natural state of unboundedness and its essential quality of clarity and luminosity cannot be disturbed by whatever is arising. In terms of view, that is the confidence that one tries to establish at the beginning, because we always tend to have some anxiety with respect to disturbing thoughts and emotions. We may think of them as enemies of meditation. We may have the attitude that if we are thinking too much, we are not meditating, and if we are thinking less, then we are meditating.

Mahamudra teachings say, however, that just because you are not thinking too much doesn't mean you are meditating, and just because you are thinking a lot, does not mean you are not meditating. It has to do with one's own experience of meditation.

If one's mind is settled, but is lacking in clarity, then one is not in a meditative state. Therefore, in Mahamudra, instead of trying to create some kind of special mental state called "the meditative state," what one tries to do is inculcate a new way of thinking called "thinking about things in terms of unity."

We think about things in terms of "appearance and emptiness," "bliss and emptiness," and "luminosity and emptiness." Even when we have an experience of bliss or luminosity, we still see that in relation to its unbounded nature and its uncreated nature. Even though what has arisen in terms of appearance is transient and will pass, nevertheless it is unbounded and uncreated in nature, the same as one's own natural state. Everything has to be seen as a unitive experience.

To emphasize that point in Mahamudra, many different kinds of words are used. One is the notion of *sahaja*[25] (Skt.), or co-emergence. We talk about such things as "co-emergent wisdom" and "co-emergent ignorance," meaning that everything, even samsaric bondage and nirvanic freedom, have to be seen as non-separable. We do not try to understand them independently of each another, but as a co-partnership; they are not in conflict. Appearance and emptiness are also not in conflict.

It is not the case that appearance leads us to delusions whereas emptiness leads to truth and reality. The appearances that we get distracted by and caught up in have the same nature as emptiness itself. The nature of appearance itself is unbounded, uncaused, and not understanding that is what has led us astray. It is not appearances that lead us astray; it is because of not understanding that appearances have the nature of being unbounded, uncreated, and, as Mahamudra teachings repeatedly emphasize, that there is equality or equanimity in all things. That is the meaning of *nyampa nyi*[26] (Tib.) which literally means evenness or equality. There is equality between thoughts and luminosity, thoughts and emptiness; it is not the case that thoughts obscure emptiness and luminosity.

Thoughts themselves are unbounded in nature; they are uncreated, because the nature of thoughts is *dharmakaya*[27] (Skt.). As the lineage prayer[28] says: *namtok ngowo chökur sungpa shin*[29] (Tib.). *Namtok* is "discursive thoughts" and *ngowo* means "nature"; *chöku* is "dharmakaya," our authentic state of being. So if we have the right view, we will see that the nature of thoughts is dharmakaya. If we understand that, then we understand appearance and emptiness also, because whatever arises in our own mind is not seen as something that will inevitably lead to delusions and add to the density of our obscurations.

To emphasize this point, many different kinds of images are given in the Mahamudra teachings. One very common example is that of the waves and the ocean. Oceans can be very turbulent and throw up huge waves which cause significant disturbances but the ocean itself, deep down, is always very still and vast. However you cannot say the waves and the ocean have a different nature; the waves have the same nature as the ocean, they are not separable. In a similar fashion, thoughts and the nature of thoughts cannot be separated. By seeing the nature of thoughts, thoughts themselves are liberated. In other words, self-liberation means if we see that the nature of thoughts themselves is emptiness and luminosity, then we have no need to get rid of those thoughts.

These are the kinds of things spoken of at the beginning of Mahamudra meditation in order to establish the view.

Working with the three aspects of the mind: nature, essence, and characteristic

The establishment of the view is also often called Ground Mahamudra, the three aspects of which are the nature of the mind, the essence of the mind, and the characteristic of the mind. We work with Ground Mahamudra in relation to these three aspects. Sometimes Western translators describe this as "one nature" or "one essence" and "different isolates" on the grounds that the term "different isolates" is more accurate. What is important though, is that emptiness and luminosity, and then phenomenal appearance, both in terms of the *subjective* experience which involves luminous emptiness and also bliss and emptiness and the *objective* experience of appearance and emptiness, should be understood together.

According to Mahayana teachings generally, and especially in teachings like Mahamudra, what stops us from seeing things clearly is our dualistic thinking. Thus it is not just the fact that we have thoughts that causes us to go astray, but it's due to seeing things in a dualistic fashion. The term in Tibetan for going astray as used in this sense is *trulpa*[30] (Tib.).

If we see appearance and emptiness, luminosity and emptiness, bliss and emptiness as not being separate but having the same nature, we are seeing things in a non-dualistic fashion.

Then, without having to cut out the discursive thoughts per se, by seeing that the discursive thoughts have the same nature as the nature of the mind itself, we see things in a non-dualistic fashion. The thoughts then become self-liberated. That is the point, and that is why the notion of *zungjuk*[31] (Tib.) is spoken of so much in Mahamudra teachings. *Zungjuk* means coming together, non-duality, so the pairing of the different things. Usually this involves the pairing of two seemingly unrelated concepts. On the one side we have things we think are more real or true, and that is paired with something else which we normally, even in Buddhist teachings, would think of as being less real or true.

An example of this would be the pairing of relative truth and absolute truth. Realizing the non-divisibility of these two truths is to really have the proper perspective on Ground Mahamudra, because the characteristic aspect of the ground represents the relative aspect. The nature and essence, in terms of unboundedness, in terms of luminosity, clarity, represent the absolute aspect; but the absolute and relative cannot be separated, because without the relative, we will have no experience to be spoken about. In this way, even the experience of our absolute nature, if we can call it that, has to be filtered through the relative, as a living, breathing individual who has such experiences and so forth. It thus has to be channeled through a particular individual's personal experience, and in doing so it is made sense of and taken on board.

Appreciating mind's creative energy

In other words, one does not simply break into some very vast, vague kind of empty space when one realizes one's authentic state, because the authentic state is realized in relation to what is also often referred to as "mind's own creative energy." This is another concept one finds used extensively in Mahamudra and Dzogchen literature. One finds terms such as *tsal*[32] (Tib.) and *nupa*[33] (Tib.) used repeatedly.

The term *tsal* refers to the mind's creative energy, meaning the unceasing thoughts, emotions, feelings, and so forth. These are not eliminated nor are they repressed or suppressed; instead they are thought of as mind's own creative energy. If understood properly, we can actually benefit from them. Not understanding them, however, leads to confusion, suffering, pain, and misery. Along with this, as we find in many Mahayana teachings, the word "skill" is used.

When we do not have the skill, the mind's creative energy is expressed in the wrong way, in a distorted fashion; it is encrusted with varieties of obsessions, fixations, graspingness, clinginess, and so on. We get bogged down and the mind's lucency, the mind's energy, becomes blocked. We are then burdened with layers of unresolved issues.

The way to have some kind of perspective on Ground Mahamudra then, is to see that the energy that comes from the unceasing thoughts, emotions, and so forth can be a good thing, and so it is not the case that we need to attempt to block them out in order to be in the natural state. If we think we need to block them then, again, we are looking at it from a dualistic point of view, and it cannot happen.

In other words, the mind's creative energy is just allowed to rise and fall. Just being with that is the best approach. Right from the beginning, Mahamudra shamatha meditation is pursued in that spirit, with that kind of attitude. One does not think of the thoughts, emotions, and feelings as clouds and that the sun of one's own true nature will come out when those clouds dissipate. In this case the clouds, handled properly, will not obscure mind's own true brilliance, one's true nature, so one does not need to worry.

Not battling thoughts

It is said that if we meditate that way, then our shamatha meditation will follow very well. Not thinking is not easy. It is not easy to block thoughts out, and trying to stop thinking takes a lot of energy. It is very exhausting and, as Mahamudra teachers have said, trying to teach the mind not to think is like trying to stop a dog from causing a commotion. Wangchuk Dorjé in his Mahamudra manual[34] gives the example of a dog, where he comments that if you put a dog on a leash and tie it to a post, it will become restless and be jumping up and down and pulling at the rope and wanting to be free. But if you let the dog loose, at the beginning it may be a little active and run around and bark, but then it will tire itself out, find a comfortable corner and just lie down and go to sleep. The implication here is that if we get too worked up, too concerned about having thoughts during meditation, and think that as soon as we sit down, our mind will go wild then conclude that we don't have the aptitude for meditation, then we are taking the wrong approach. It is having *those* thoughts, the running commentary, that causes disruption; not the thoughts that arose in the first place.

If we don't try to stop the thoughts from arising, then the thoughts will move on, because it is in their nature to move on, and that is something that we need to pay attention to. That is how it is put, that if we just let the thoughts pass, they will pass, because thoughts by nature are transient. But if we are trying to get rid of the thoughts, then this is an expression of what in Buddhist teaching is called "mental fixation." We become fixated on those thoughts and end up struggling with them and, by doing so, they begin to proliferate and become more profuse.

Thoughts don't lessen simply because we don't want to think, or we don't want certain thoughts. They don't get scared off because we think, "I don't want these thoughts," or, "I hate these thoughts." Not only are the thoughts not intimidated, they become even more unruly and assertive. A gentler approach to meditation is thus required, one which emphasizes the notion of acceptance and accommodation rather than trying to create a certain kind of meditative state.

What is involved, then, is having the willingness to work with the whole gamut of our experiences be they good or bad, pleasant or unpleasant. And by having that openness, automatically the tension is reduced; the anxiety one feels is lessened. The next time a disturbing thought arises one is less disturbed by it. Even if disturbing thoughts do arise, because our attitude is not one of disapproval, we then become less disturbed and are much more at ease with what is going on in our mind. We become friendlier with our mind instead of fighting with it. Fighting with our mind is also one of the main causes of our suffering, pain, and misery.

Being able to be with one's mind irrespective of what it throws up, there is greater self-acceptance, and meditation becomes a lot easier. We have a tendency to want our meditation mind to deliver the goods, so to speak. When it doesn't deliver, we become upset and may even begin to become suspicious of our own mind. We may even go so far as to think that our mind is up to something behind our back, trying to undermine us, to sneak up on us and throw us an unwanted surprise. When this happens, of course we feel very upset. Meditation practiced with acceptance and accommodation instead is a way of making friends with our mind, being able to work with our mind. If we have the willingness to do that, then the mind also becomes more responsive and easier to deal with.

Being skillful

Again, this is an extension of the Mahayana use of skillful means. We have to be skillful, we have to think in terms of what works, not only in terms of what might be a good idea, or a good thing to do. There are many good things, but sometimes doing those good things doesn't work unless one is skillful in carrying them out. That is the key, and dealing with one's own mind is no different. Shamatha meditation is definitely pursued with that kind of attitude. The tranquility of shamatha then arises from not having too much tension between one's self and one's mind and, as the teachings say, we should not think of thoughts and emotions as our enemies.

So far in discussing the approach of self-liberation, we have mainly concentrated on Ground Mahamudra, which has to do with realizing our own authentic state of being. The practices of shamatha and vipashyana are done in order for us to realize that state. In many ways, then, the Mahamudra approach to meditation and practice is not really about cultivation. Cultivation implies we are lacking something, so then we cultivate the missing attributes or qualities. In Mahamudra, though, it is more about finding these qualities in ourselves. Through the Mahamudra approach we can come to appreciate that many of the qualities we need in order to become enlightened, to free ourselves from suffering and pain and confusion, already exist within ourselves.

Realizing the ground is the fruit

This approach of self-liberation is then quite unique and, as has been mentioned, distinct from other Buddhist approaches. Sometimes the alternative names for the other approaches listed earlier vary. At times the term *causal yana* is used. *Yana*[35] (Skt.) means "vehicle," and the *causal yana* refers to the traditional, conventional Mahayana approach. The Mahamudra approach is sometimes called the *fruition yana*, emphasizing Mahamudra, the fruit which is already present.

In Mahamudra terminology we talk about Ground, Path, and Fruition Mahamudra, but what we realize is that Fruition Mahamudra and Ground Mahamudra are the same. While the fruit of Mahamudra is realized, what one actually realizes is Ground Mahamudra. The notion of Ground Mahamudra is emphasized at the beginning, though, because we haven't realized or had experience of Mahamudra and so need some conceptual perspective on what it is and how to have experience of it.

Path Mahamudra has to do with the practices of shamatha and vipashyana, which allow us to realize the ground as the fruit. Ground Mahamudra is not the starting point with Fruition Mahamudra seen as another state that one attains, but understanding or realizing Ground Mahamudra is the Fruition Mahamudra.

The Path:
Shamatha and Vipashyana

When we practice Mahamudra with the practices of shamatha and vipashyana, different kinds of attitudes are encouraged. We find repeated injunctions to develop what is called "the attitude of neither acceptance nor rejection." When we are practicing, if negative thoughts arise, if discursive thoughts arise, if strong emotions arise, we should not immediately react to these by thinking, "Oh, this is bad, I should not have these experiences." If we have good or comforting or inspiring experiences during meditation, then we should not get overjoyed and think, "Oh, I'm getting somewhere, my meditation experiences have been very positive lately. It's a positive sign, I'm blessed." If we continue to deal with our meditative experiences in that way, then, according to Mahamudra teachings, we will not progress very much because we will be driven by hope and fear. We are hoping for wonderful things to happen and we are fearful they will not, or that bad things might happen.

In Tibetan the phrase *panglang redok dang dralwa*[36] is used. *Pang* is "to renounce," "to give up"; *lang* means "to cultivate." *Re* is short for *rewa* which is "hope" and *dok* is short for *dokpa* which means "fear." Finally, *dralwa* means "to be free of." Altogether then, this means we try to approach Path Mahamudra meditation by being free of notions of acceptance, rejection, and hope and fear.

If we get bogged down by thoughts of what to cultivate, what to renounce and give up, and we get caught up in hoping things will be working out well and fearing they will not, these become distractions and impediments to our path. Instead of producing shamatha tranquility, they disturb our mind. This is one of the main instructions given and a very important key part of the practice.

It is also suggested that if we get bogged down with thoughts of acceptance, rejection, hope and fear, we also drive a wedge between time now and time in the future. We start thinking that something good has to happen in the future, or that something bad is going to happen in the future. The main attitude one should have is the willingness to work with whatever is arising in one's mind now, whatever one is experiencing at any given time. This is what one should be focusing on, rather than thinking about what these experiences may mean or be symbolic of or be leading one into, in relation to the future.

Letting go of the running commentary

We try to interpret our experiences all the time, and give them a lot of commentary. To a large extent, how our experiences are appropriated, made sense of, given significance and meaning, depends upon our mood, or even the time of the day. This is also something that we have to keep in mind. It is not only that we form interpretations in terms of things external to us, but we also interpret what we ourselves are going through at any given time. As soon as we start to conceptualize and attempt to understand what is really going on, we lose touch with the bare experience. In other words, the bare experience becomes shrouded by our interpretive accretions. You might say we put layers of commentary on what is experienced.

In Mahamudra we try to stay with the experience, and if we stay with the experience, then we are going to interpret our experiences less in terms of whether they are a good experiences or bad experiences. In order to follow the Path Mahamudra we need to refrain from evaluating everything we experience. Simply thinking an experience is bad because of our own confusion and habits of mind, does not mean it is bad. Conversely, just because we think certain experiences are good, does not necessarily mean they are good. We should consider these things so that we don't jump ahead and start conceptualizing about what we are experiencing.

We need to try to have some sense of openness by thinking about things like this. An experience that we may have thought was not very good could, in time, with deeper understanding, deeper appreciation of meditation, and the benefit of hindsight, be thought of in fact as beneficial. At the time, though, it may have been upsetting or uncomfortable, or even confronting. Just because something is pleasant, doesn't necessarily mean it is good for us, and just because something is a bit confronting or unpleasant, doesn't mean it is bad for us. Even in life generally that happens to be true, of course. We could keep out of a lot of trouble if we follow that rule.

It is extremely important to keep an open mind. In that way, one tries to meditate, to practice shamatha. It is said that if we approach things in this way and are open to varieties of experiences, then experiences will rise and fall, rise and fall and we will be less given to distractions and disturbances. A very common example used for how to deal with the mind is to describe it as being like an undisturbed pond. Vigorous use of mindfulness and emptiness is seen as disturbing or stirring the pond. If one stirs a pond, all the sediment at the bottom will come to the top and, in one's confused attempt to keep the pond clean, it gets murky and muddy. But if the pond is let be, left alone, then all the sediment sinks to the bottom and the pond will be clear. Doing less will bring the most benefit, and doing more results in less benefit.

Maintaining awareness whether the mind is stable or in movement

The main thing is to be able to stay with whatever is arising and if we do that, we are maintaining our awareness, which is the key to meditation. If we practice awareness in relation to a wide range of emotions, feelings, and experiences, then we will develop a certain ability to maintain awareness under many different circumstances. If we can only maintain awareness when our mind is sufficiently calm and not when the mind becomes slightly agitated, then our meditation is partial. Our ability to practice awareness is not well-established, because a slight disturbance is enough to snuff out the awareness.

Again, an example is given to describe this. Think of a strong gust of wind as disturbing discursive thoughts and a small flame as awareness. If the flame is very small, the wind will almost automatically wipe it out; the flame does not have much chance. But if the flame is sufficiently strong, the wind actually encourages the flame to blaze even more, rather than putting it out. In a similar way, it is said that if the meditator is able to harness awareness, likened to the flame, and maintain it even if there is a great deal going on in the mind, it is like the wind and the flame helping each other. Strong emotions, thoughts, and feelings are not then anathema to the flame of awareness. The flame is actually encouraged and gets stronger, just as with training in physical exercise, the more we train, the more we are able to put up with physical stress. If we use awareness under a variety of circumstances and situations, then we are able to maintain shamatha tranquility. Otherwise, when the mind is calm, awareness is present, and when it is not calm, awareness is not present.

Nowhere is it said that you cannot maintain awareness when the mind is in a state of movement, as it is called. That is the other key thing to remember, that we can maintain awareness in a state of movement and in a state of non-movement. Both are mentioned in Mahamudra literature on shamatha and they are called "the meditative state of non-movement" and "the meditative state of movement."

Movement refers to when there are thoughts, feelings, emotions, and so forth rushing through the mind. There is a phrase in Mahamudra vocabulary: *né gyu rik sum*[37] (Tib.). The terms used in the phrase are *né*, which means when the mind is stable, *gyu*, when the mind is in a state of movement, and *rik* means awareness, which may be more familiar in full as *rikpa*. This phrase refers to being able to maintain awareness whether the mind is in a stable state or in a state of movement.

This is the key to how we establish shamatha stability. We don't do so by trying to deliberately reduce the activity in the mind but by trying to maintain awareness, even in a state of movement. This is, again, a very important notion. Otherwise our meditation becomes partial and our awareness fickle; it can't be properly established because it doesn't have sufficient strength to maintain itself when the mind is in a state of movement.

Movement means when there are thoughts and emotions and feelings arising in the mind. What this means then is we don't have to think that the mind should be empty of thoughts or feelings or emotions to be in a meditative state. It doesn't matter whether we have thoughts or no thoughts; that is not the key. Instead, the key is to maintain awareness.

Strengthening our awareness

To establish this kind of awareness in Mahamudra as part of shamatha meditation an exercise is given. If our mind is a bit agitated, we try to stabilize it by watching the breath, for example, or whatever is going to help us achieve that. We try to calm the mind down and create some stability. If the mind is already somewhat stable, we deliberately think of something or even give rise to some strong emotion and then return to a stable mind. We continue to repeat the exercise, so that we are going from stability to movement and movement to stability, then stability to movement and movement to stability, again and again, always trying to keep mental awareness. That is how we try to make our awareness stronger, so that we get used to maintaining awareness even when there is movement in the mind, not just when the mind is stable. This is what *né gyu rik sum* refers to.

These exercises are used as a very effective method to maintain awareness, no matter what is happening. In stillness, we try to create movement, and in movement we try to create stillness, and if we do that, we may develop what is called "the balance between stability and clarity." If we are able to maintain proper awareness, then there will not be too much clarity, because if there is too much clarity, this leads to agitation.

If there is not enough clarity, then having too much stability leads to dullness of the mind. When we go back and forth from movement to stillness and stillness to movement, we learn about this balance. This is called *necha* and *selcha*[38] (Tib.). *Né* means "stability" and *cha* means "portion," so *necha* means "the portion of mind which is stable" and as *sel* means "luminosity" or "clarity," *selcha* means "the clarity portion." We have to try to have balance between these two so that too much clarity does not lead to agitation, and too much stability does not lead to dullness and stupor. The portions have to be maintained in a balanced state. This is not to say that we won't have more clarity sometimes and at other times a bit more stability; they don't have to be in exact equal portions, so to speak. Nevertheless there has to be some kind of balance.

We may also develop that balance if we are meditating in the way we have been discussing, using movement and stillness together, and again not thinking that stillness is something that is really good and movement is a bad thing. If we are not thinking like that and we try to bring harmony between the two, our ability to maintain stability and clarity will increase. That is what shamatha practice of meditation involves.

While I am giving you the essentials here, to do this kind of meditation you do have to study with a qualified lama; you can't do this kind of practice just by reading a book. While I am sure you know that already, we have a duty to inform people of that again and again, as well. In our tradition we are instructed to do this, so I am passing that on. These are the essential instructions normally given to gain stability of the mind, because the main point of shamatha is to stabilize the mind.

To recapitulate, we stabilize the mind by harmonizing the movement versus stillness by trying not to get caught up in thoughts of acceptance and rejection, hope and fear and so forth, and, most importantly, by trying to maintain this balance between stability and mental clarity. When the mind becomes more stabilized that way, we gain shamatha stability.

The insights of vipashyana

Based on that, we are then introduced to the Mahamudra path of vipashyana, which means insight. In Mahamudra practice this is done through what we call "introduction of the nature of the mind." This has several steps:

(i) Seeing all appearances as mind

First, we try to think that everything we experience, even in terms of the so-called "objective material world," is dependent on the mind. We have to think of the mind as being an extremely powerful instrument. In this way, the mind is not seen as something that simply receives information, but as a creative agent which actually constructs the world that we live in.

Sometimes people think these teachings are saying that everything is literally created by the mind but I don't think we have to go that far. It might be sufficient that we think we can only have the experience of anything, including physical entities and the natural world itself, through and from our mind.

We cannot step outside the mind and have an objective perspective on the world. We cannot go outside our mind and ask, "Is my mind reflecting the objective world correctly or not?" Any kind of world we experience can only be experienced in relation to how our own mind is structured. Therefore the first insight, the first introduction that one is given is called "to see all appearances as the mind."

When the word "appearances" is used in this kind of literature, it does not simply mean the sensory appearances or what sense data affords us in terms of what we are experiencing. It does not just mean visual, auditory, or olfactory appearances, and so on, but also what is internal. Our thoughts, emotions, feelings, and sensations are thus also described as appearances in this kind of literature.

When the literature states, "appearances are not separate from the mind," we try to understand that. Various kinds of exercises are given in this regard, such as using one's sensory impressions and trying to see a tree or a house or a human being and staying with that without any kind of conceptual gloss so that one is just being with that experience. Then one realizes that it is very difficult to separate the sense object perceived and the sensing subject, the subjective mind; it is not easy to draw a clear-cut demarcation line.

In order to see that everything that arises in the mind is also "appearances," we deliberately give rise to contrasting emotions even if we are not feeling strong emotions. This shows us how the mind can actually create our mood. We can make ourselves feel quite low and unhappy, or we can make ourselves feel uplifted and joyful. An example could be that we think about something that will make us sad, imagining we have lost something that we really cherish, love, or something that was really precious to us. We imagine that we have lost that, and we feel that sense of loss acutely. We then follow that with a contrasting emotion. We think about something that would make us feel really happy, something that would make us really joyous—something that we desire and want to chase after. Then we think that we have attained or received whatever it is that we desire and give rise to the appropriate feeling and emotion. We feel that, and then observe the contrast between the two emotions.

Through this also, we begin to gain some insight into our mind in terms of appearances being mind. Without any change in what we consider to be external, the mind can make things up. This directly impacts on how we are feeling, on the thoughts going through our mind and the sort of mood we have managed to put ourselves into.

In that way, we realize that even though we always think that our moods and so forth are totally dependent on things external to us, nevertheless when we pay attention to the mind itself, we begin to see how it is actually contributing to these experiences. While we think it is the other people who make us angry or sad or happy or whatever, and that external circumstances and situations lead us to go through all kinds of emotional upheavals, it is not just in what we consider external.

To a large part, even *what* we see is also determined by the mind. It depends on our habits, our character, our personality, our mood at a given time, our belief systems, and the value we attach to what we are experiencing. All these things go towards seeing the world in a particular, individually-tailored way. Far from being in direct contact with an objective world, we are directly responsible for creating this world that we are in contact with.

That is the first step, the first insight that one tries to develop through vipashyana meditation. By contemplating this kind of thing, there is the added benefit of allowing us to know that we are not victims of circumstances. It is not just the external circumstances and situations that are responsible for our level of enjoyment or lack of it in life, but it is we who actually decide; it is in our own hands. So seeing appearances as mind is a very important first step; it is the first stage of vipashyana, introducing appearance as mind.

(ii) Seeing mind's nature as emptiness

Next, we go into the mind itself and look at this mind that has the capacity to produce strong emotions and feelings. We look at the mind that develops strong opinions and very dogmatic views on various issues along with all the biases and prejudices that go with these. If we look at the mind itself, we realize that the mind is actually not something we can grasp at; it is not easy to get a handle on the mind.

So with the second introduction, the mind is introduced as having the nature of emptiness. "The nature of the mind is emptiness," as it is said, is then the second insight. The mind's nature is empty because when we look into the nature of the mind, it is not something; we do not manage to get a grip on it, so it is elusive. That elusiveness, itself, reveals its true nature. That is a positive insight; it is not a mere absence of things.

Seeing the mind's true nature in that way frees us from all kinds of mental constrictions. Because of our unceasing thoughts, our mind becomes very tight, very bound, rigid. When we really look into that mind in itself, it is not something that reveals itself as having tangible form, and that in itself is liberating.

The mind's creative nature lies in the fact that it does not have a fixed nature as such, yet manifests in so many ways. If mind had a fixed nature, then its creativity would be very limited. It would only be able to manifest in a fixed number of forms because it would not be in its nature to manifest in other ways. But the mind's nature is not fixed and is instead empty, as we say in the lineage prayer, *chiyang mayin chiryang charwa la*[39] (Tib.), "It is not anything in itself, yet it appears, manifests, in so many different forms." That then is the second introduction.

(iii) Seeing emptiness as spontaneously-established phenomena

By seeing mind's own nature as emptiness and then seeing everything else—all the appearances—as having emptiness as their nature rather than a fixed nature, then one sees that everything is *lhundrup*[40] in Tibetan, which means "spontaneously-established." Spontaneously-established is a very clumsy expression, but it means that we think of things less in terms of causes and conditions, as we normally would with respect to phenomena, and more in terms of manifesting spontaneously.

Normally, we look at things and try to find explanations in terms of causality, asking for example, "Why did something or other happen?" and concluding, "because of something else." But having understood something about emptiness and seeing emptiness itself as being the nature of everything, then one is not looking at things purely in causal terms but as manifesting spontaneously.

When varieties of things come together, then things change form, things manifest differently; the display of the phenomena, as we say, occurs. It is as if there is dynamism, vitality, in how the phenomenal world is seen. It is no longer seen in terms of "thing-ness."

Our normal way of perceiving things is to think they have a certain substance and, on top of that, particular attributes, such as shape, size, color, and so forth. We thus think in terms of things having certain essences and this is the essentialist view. But by thinking in terms of spontaneously-established phenomena, we are thinking of things in a different way.

Things appear and disappear at a very rapid pace, and because everything is happening at such a fast pace, we do not view things as static. It is more that different things are positioned in a certain way and then they mutually interact with each other, causing further different things to come into being. In any case, this is called "spontaneously-established" phenomena, and emptiness is then seen as part of spontaneously-established phenomena, which is the next insight.

(iv) Seeing spontaneously-established phenomena as self-liberated

Since we are seeing all the appearances, external and internal, sensory and non-sensory, from a non-essentialist, non-substantialist point of view, and in terms of vibrant dynamism, we see them as self-liberated.

They are right in their own way; there is nothing wrong with them. There is no problem with anything that is going on. From this point of view, vibrant phenomena are not seen as illusory or something of that nature, but perceived for what they are. As it is said in the teachings, one realizes that nothing has to be added and nothing needs to be taken out of that reality, which is also a very important Mahamudra concept that is often used.

One does not need to add anything, nor does one need to take anything out to make things better. Everything that happens is happening just as it should. If we have that insight, then there is no room for bondage so, therefore, everything is self-liberated. As soon as things arise, they dissipate; they appear, disappear, appear and disappear.

The idea then is that if the Mahamudra practitioner is transformed, all these mental imprints leave only very faint traces. There are no karmic imprints to bear; one is not bogged down by one's karmic inheritance and history. Karmic imprints are hardly created because such an individual is not caught up in fixation. Whatever appears disappears, because everything is liberated.

As we know, in Buddhism, a lot of our misery comes from mental fixation: we hang onto things; we latch onto or seize things, our experiences, and so forth. Then, due to our confusion, we do not see that the experiences themselves can never remain the same and are always in a state of dynamism. A stasis is then created which does not leave room for development and creativity. We get bogged down by our karmic imprints and this, as the tradition states, leads to impure perceptions, *ma dakpai nangwa*[41] (Tib.). But if we see *lhundrup*, if we see that things are in a state of dynamism and vibrancy, then that leads to *dakpai nangwa*[42] or *daknang* for short, which means "pure perception."

It is thus not the perception itself that is to be blamed, but how we perceive things. It is about whether we perceive things with a very tenacious sense of fixation and clinginess or whether we see things differently, in terms of vibrancy and as being in a state of constant creative movement. That perception is called "pure perception". That is the final insight that one gains in terms of vipashyana meditation.

In Mahamudra vipashyana meditation, this series of insights is specifically mentioned. The insights are mentioned in the order described: first seeing appearances as mind; then the mind as empty; then emptiness as spontaneously-established phenomena; then seeing spontaneously-established phenomena as self-liberated.

We have now covered a brief overview of the insights of vipashyana.

The non-separability of appearance and reality

The concept of spontaneously-established phenomena is very important because, in Mahamudra, the real insight lies in understanding the non-separability of emptiness and appearance, or reality and appearance. In our mistaken state we think of appearance and reality as being separate. We also think reality is completely real, whereas appearance is not real and reality hides behind it, or something of that nature. We learn from these teachings this is not the case, that appearance does not hide reality.

To see the nature of the appearance is to see reality. It is thus not the case that we are deluded because we perceive appearances, but we are deluded because we do not perceive the nature of appearances. If we perceive the nature of appearances, then we will also perceive reality so, as pointed out in the teachings, to see appearance and reality to be non-divisible or inseparable is to see things in a non-dualistic fashion.

If we separate appearance and reality, however, we are not free of duality. If we think appearance is something bad and reality is something good, then we are still trapped in dualistic perception. We are thinking of appearance and reality as separate: reality as something we perceive with our wisdom eye or mind and appearance as perceived with our dualistic deluded mind. To see the non-separability is the profound insight one gains through practice of vipashyana. As the lineage prayer states:

> *chiyang mayin chiryang charwala*
> *mangak rölpa charwai gomchenla*
> *khordé yerme tokpar jin-gyi lop*[43]

This means "while not being anything in themselves, varieties of things appear, and these appearances are uninterrupted." They are uninterrupted and *rölpa*[44] (Tib.), sometimes translated into English as "play of the mind." We then get the expression "uninterrupted play of the mind." The expression *rölpa charwa*[45] also has the connotation of enjoyment.

Putting it all together, it includes the notion of being able to fully enjoy the display of phenomena. Realizing the nature of the mind or realizing the nature of the reality does not lead to non-enjoyment of the appearances; instead, it actually leads to enjoyment of appearances. The concept of *rölpa* is also connected with one other word referred to earlier, and that is the notion of *tsal*, "creative power."

We see everything we experience as *rölpa*, as some kind of phenomenal display we can actually enjoy without fixation. Whatever we experience in terms of inner appearances, we see as manifestation of the mind's own creative energy, as *tsal*.

Without having to block the thoughts and emotions and so forth arising in the mind, without fixation we see everything as mind's own creative energy. And, by doing so, we experience bliss. Whether we are experiencing outer or inner phenomena, outer or inner appearances, we have the experience of bliss.

Normally what happens is that out of habit, when we see, smell, taste, or touch something, we get fixated on whatever sensory engagement occurs. Also, in terms of our inner experiences, the same thing happens. If we have a thought popping into our mind, we can't let that thought pass, we have to do something about it. We have to think about it, and thinking about thinking is what we do a lot of the time. We think one thought, and then we think about what we have thought, and then we think about what we have thought in terms of what we have thought, and so on.

Bliss comes not because nothing is arising in the mind or one is not paying attention to the phenomenal display, but when whatever one experiences does not give rise to fixation. Then there is bliss, *dechen*[46] (Tib.), but *dechen gyunché mé*[47] (Tib.) is also spoken of. *Gyunché* means "interruption" and *mé* means "not," so *dechen gyunché mé* means "uninterrupted bliss." You can enjoy what you are seeing, smelling, tasting, and touching and you can enjoy what is going through your mind because none of these things give rise to fixation.

Because you are not grasping at them, your experiences remain fluid, vibrant, and vital and they are not arrested. You are not trying to capture these things with your over-conceptualization, as we say, with *vikalpa*[48] (Skt.), which means "conceptual, discursive thoughts." The word for this in Tibetan is *namtok*.[49] The other word used is *prapancha*[50] (Skt.) and *tröpa*[51] in Tibetan, which means "conceptual elaboration." If we are caught in these things, then our fixation strengthens and our mind becomes static and loses its pliancy, as we would say in Buddhism. In other words, the mind becomes less workable; it becomes rigid. Conversely, as fixation begins to loosen then everything we experience is more enjoyable.

Shamatha and vipashyana combined

If we do our practice in this way so that we are not thinking of either shamatha or vipashyana alone, but combining shamatha with vipashyana practice, we have the stability of shamatha as well as the clarity of vipashyana. These different kinds of meditation have separate functions. As practitioners, with shamatha we learn how to stabilize the mind, and with vipashyana we begin to sharpen our mind so that some kind of cognitive transformation takes place in us.

It is possible to meditate simply by dealing with thoughts and emotions. We can practice meditation in such a way as to be able to reduce negative feelings and encourage more positive feelings. We can learn to have more positive emotions and reduce the negative forms of emotion. From a Buddhist point of view, if we have not practiced vipashyana and tried to see things differently from how we normally look at things, then, because we are not seeing things correctly, we will not be transformed. In order to gain enlightenment we need to have insight, and insight means we have to see things differently.

That is the key, and we need to keep that in mind. Otherwise, as we continue to practice our meditation, doing shamatha and vipashyana and so on—especially if we are not doing vipashyana correctly—then even if we have meditative experiences, these can lead to what is called "going astray" or deviating from the Path Mahamudra. These kinds of instructions also feature prominently in Mahamudra teachings.

Maintaining the Mahamudra Attitude

There are five perspectives we need to maintain in the teachings to avoid deviation:

- Correcting mistaken ideas about objects
- Correcting mistaken ideas about time
- Correcting mistaken ideas about the essence
- Correcting mistaken ideas about nature
- Correcting mistaken ideas about knowledge

These five mistaken ideas are important to think about, because we have to have a proper perspective. They are considered a way of maintaining a Mahamudra philosophical attitude when it comes to the practice.

Correcting mistaken ideas about objects

"Correcting mistaken ideas about objects" refers to not using Mahamudra meditation practice in a way that involves thinking about what we should cultivate or reject. In other words, it means that we should try to have a more positive view of negative emotions and feelings.

We should not think that negative feelings and negative emotions are poisonous, as has sometimes been said. Instead, we should think that what are known as the negative poisons, which are negative thoughts and emotions, have the potential to be liberated as well. Just as with the tantric or esoteric approach of

Buddhism, we can learn a lot from our poisons, from our negative thoughts and emotions.

We should not think that we can only profit from positive emotions, positive feelings, and that negative emotions and negative feelings are totally useless with nothing to teach us. This is something we have to think about rather than, again, viewing things in a dualistic fashion. Through taking a skillful approach, we realize that what we normally regard as poisons are not shackles, but can be used constructively.

We think about things in that way and extend it to consideration of virtues and vices. One approach is to think that virtues will lead us to happiness and nirvanic liberation, while vices will lead to unhappiness and keep us entrapped in samsaric bondage. From the Mahamudra perspective, though, we know that if we can handle them correctly, we could even profit from things that we would normally be harmed by. This is also called *nyönmong lam khyer* [52] in Tibetan, which means "taking the poisons as the path."

The poisons are thus used to further our progress, rather than us thinking they are a bad thing. As many Mahayana teachings say, it is like using manure as fertilizer. The idea is that you use the manure, namely the five poisons of excessive desire, anger, jealousy, pride and ignorance, on the field of body. By scattering it you are actually fertilizing the field of body, "body" meaning the enlightened state. That is one philosophical attitude one should have.

Correcting mistaken ideas about time

When we have embarked on the Mahamudra path, we do not think in terms of ourselves as lowly human beings and the Buddha as a totally enlightened and superior being. In other words, we do not think there is a big gap separating the deluded state and the enlightened state. We do not think of the enlightened state as something one attains in the future and the deluded state as the state one is in.

Here, instead, what we should be thinking is that the state we want to attain is the state we are already in, even though we don't know about it. As Rangjung Dorjé has stated in his Mahamudra prayer, "by not recognizing 'it', we wander about endlessly in samsara; by knowing about 'it', we attain nirvanic liberation."[53] Here, "it" refers to our natural state, our true authentic state of being.

The difference between the buddha and the non-buddha, then, lies not in terms of who they are but has to do with whether the individual has woken up to their own true state or not.

So a buddha does not become enlightened in the sense of renouncing a certain state and then achieving another kind of state in the future. In any case, one should not think too much about "now" and "then," but instead think about attaining buddhahood or enlightenment in relation to one's own nature, one's true authentic state of being. That, again, is a helpful philosophical attitude to have. By having these kinds of thoughts, we will be able to practice Mahamudra shamatha and vipashyana meditation more easily. If we don't, we will have a problem with correctly implementing these practices.

Correcting mistaken ideas about the essence

"Essence" here refers to the essence of the mind. What this means is that, from the Mahamudra point of view, we should not think that a buddha possesses a wisdom mind whereas we do not, and that our mind is imbued with ignorance and so on but a buddha's mind is imbued with wisdom. If we think that way, then it means that we believe there are essential differences between what a buddha's mind is, and what a samsaric mind is. Again, it is a big mistake to think like this because there is no essential difference between the two.

We talked earlier about the three aspects of one's being: that its nature is emptiness, unbounded, unrestricted, free; the essence is luminous clarity, lucidity; and the characteristic of the mind is the thoughts and emotions and so forth that continue to flow through us.

The only difference between the mind of a buddha and that of a samsaric being lies in not understanding how these different aspects of one's being interrelate, and in getting carried away by the thoughts and emotions and so on that surge through our mind. But if we understand the interrelationship, then there is no difference.

A buddha's mind is not different from ours then, because a buddha's mind also has the nature of being unbounded, free, and so on, and the essential quality of a buddha's mind is also luminous clarity.

Next we consider a buddha's compassionate response or, in other words, how a buddha's mind operates in relation to dealing with other beings and interacting with the world.

A buddha's approach and conduct relate to wisdom activity. As mentioned earlier, we speak about a buddha having five wisdoms: wisdom of accomplishment; wisdom of equanimity; wisdom of discrimination; mirror-like wisdom; and wisdom of the natural state. A buddha's mind operates in varieties of ways. On one level, for example, a buddha sees the equanimity of all things because a buddha knows that everything has the same nature. As we say, there is a diversity of things but one taste, with that taste being emptiness, or reality. Reality is all-pervasive and does not discriminate; everything is shot through with the same reality. So a buddha has that ability. On the other hand, however, where necessary, a buddha uses the wisdom of discrimination.

A buddha is also able to use their wisdom mind like a mirror, reflecting all things in it and taking it all in. It is our normal habit to exercise selective attention, so we take in certain things and leave a lot out. Earlier, we discussed at length the editing process we have going on all the time, in terms of what we take in and what we leave out. What this means is that a great deal gets left out but a buddha, in their unbiased state, is able to have a wide panoramic view of all things. A buddha is able to exercise their mind that way, and this corresponds to the uninterrupted thoughts and emotions and feelings that arise in us in deluded form.

In terms of the mind's nature and functions then, we have to say that perhaps on the functional level there may be some difference but, in terms of nature and essence, there is no difference. When one attains buddhahood, there is no change in terms of how one sees the nature and essence of one's own state of being. Also, one realizes that whatever one experiences has the same nature as the nature of one's authentic state, so that is one perspective we need to adopt.

Correcting mistaken ideas about the nature

"Correcting mistaken ideas about the nature" refers to how, as a psychophysical embodiment in our non-awakened state, we relate to our psychophysical constituents. We have the sensory apparatus, or *ayatana*[54] (Skt.) and five psychophysical constituents, called *skandha*[55] (Skt.): form, feeling, perceptual experience, disposition, and consciousness. The idea is that in our true nature, these experiences are also not separate from reality-as-such; as we were saying before, everything is permeated by the same reality.

Although experience is diverse and far-reaching, nevertheless everything we experience, if understood properly, is imbued with the same nature. We should avoid thinking that in the deluded state, deluded experiences are not permeated by the same nature as that of non-deluded experiences. Instead, we should keep in mind that the same nature pervades through all layers of experience and all levels of being. That too is a very important perspective to keep. If we are not thinking like that, then, while meditating, we may still tend towards thinking certain experiences we encounter are "bad" while some "good" experiences are something different. We will discuss this a little later in the context of dealing with meditative experiences.

Correcting mistaken ideas about knowledge

The next perspective we should adopt to help prevent us falling into old bad habits is correcting mistaken ideas about knowledge. This refers to the need to think about knowledge itself. We try to go to the source of all knowledge, so to speak.

The source of all knowledge, all insights, and all thoughts of wisdom is self-cognizing awareness, the intrinsic awareness present in us. We should think of that as the most important thing and not get fixated on particular types of knowledge that we may have accumulated, especially of a conceptual or intellectual kind. This doesn't mean these have no value, as sometimes they are very beneficial.

The knowledge that allows us to see into the nature of things, though, is the one that is most beneficial, rather than knowledge which is simply informative. If something is informative, it may be helpful, but that kind of knowledge has no limit. On the other hand, having the kind of knowledge that comes from seeing into the nature of things, how things actually exist, the true state of affairs, can free us. Understanding this then is a key thing.

When we are meditating, we are not just trying to accumulate knowledge; instead, we are trying to gain knowledge into things. If reality is all-pervasive and penetrating, then it stands to reason that by understanding that reality, we will know that everything has that nature. As has been said in the teachings, in order to realize that all bamboo stems are hollow inside, we simply look inside one stem in a grove; we don't have to systematically chop down the whole grove to make sure the whole grove contains hollow stems. In other words, trying to realize intrinsic awareness is the key, because realizing intrinsic awareness will allow us to see into the nature of all things. This is a different kind of knowledge or insight than one that comes from understanding things individually, in terms of how they operate or how they come into being, and so forth.

That too is a very important thing to remember otherwise we may even think that doing meditation is a way of accumulating more knowledge. It is not so much that we are gaining more knowledge as deepening the insight. It is the same insight but it just becomes deeper, more profound, more penetrating, and so forth; it is not as if one is gaining extra knowledge as one goes along. That is an important distinction to make, and one which will also help us avoid going astray.

There are exercises in Mahamudra vipashyana meditation where we use analytical skill. As part of the introduction of the mind, for example, when we try to see that the nature of the mind is emptiness, we do exercises that involve seeing what the mind is like, asking ourselves such things as whether the mind has any of the specific attributes or qualities that we normally attach to things. Normally, we think of things in terms of having a certain shape, size, weight, color, and so on but when we look at the mind, we find it is not like that. By looking at the mind in different ways we realize that the mind doesn't have any real fixed nature. When we are doing that kind of exercise, however, even though we are using analytical skill, the purpose is again to awaken that intrinsic awareness which, for want of a better expression, is innate.

Maintaining our sense of basic confidence

We have now completed a general, brief summary of the kinds of attitudes one needs to keep while practicing shamatha and vipashyana meditation from a Mahamudra perspective. If we remind ourselves to keep these attitudes, they will serve us well. They will help us stay on course with the practice of meditation and curb our tendency to think that as soon as disturbances arise while doing shamatha and vipashyana, our meditation has gone to waste. They will help us not lose courage or hope.

Our sense of basic confidence, at least from the Mahamudra point of view, is not necessarily based on a specific thing we can build our confidence on. Instead, we have confidence in ourselves because in our true nature we are unbounded, free, and our own true nature is untarnished or unblemished.

If we try to maintain that kind of confidence, then even when our meditation fluctuates or we have different kinds of meditative experiences, we do not follow those things too closely, and our fixation lessens. We will therefore be happier with our meditation and feel that no matter what happens, the meditation is good, we are profiting from it.

When disturbing thoughts arise, we may not react in a bad way but think of them as being useful. If we think of negative emotions and mental states as nutrients or fertilizer, we can feel that everything has something to teach us and we can gain as much insight into these negative things as into positive things. After all, both positive experiences and negative experiences are marked by the same reality.

The word, Mahamudra, actually represents that idea; *maha* means "great" and *mudra* means "seal." What it means is that everything is marked with the great seal, and the great seal is the union of intrinsic awareness and emptiness.

Everything is permeated by the reality of emptiness which we realize through intrinsic awareness. When a monarch puts a seal on a document, that document carries authority to the extremities of their domain. So, in a similar way, everything is sealed with the same reality. The idea of authority is included as well, since everything is under the dominion of that reality. To bolster that kind of realization we try to maintain the attitudes we have been discussing and, if we are deviating or going astray, we try to remind ourselves of them and come back to having a more conducive, beneficial approach to our practices.

Experiences and Realization

Having discussed the attitudes we, as meditators, should take to stay with our practice and make it work better, we will now go on to talk about Fruition Mahamudra in terms of meditative experiences and meditative realization. In Buddhist teachings, especially in this type of teaching, a distinction is made between meditative experiences and meditative realization. This is because meditative experiences are always accompanied by strong feelings or emotions or strong physical sensations. Meditative realization, on the other hand, although it may be accompanied by feelings and so forth, is more cognitive in nature. As such, it has more to do with insight than some form of moving experience. Meditative experiences also fluctuate, as one does not consistently have the same kind of experience, even if one has advanced somewhat as a meditator. One cannot expect to continue to have strong experiences, and a lot of the problems that meditators may have come from this expectation.

Being able to distinguish between experience and realization is seen as a very important step towards making understanding more profound. One could have quite a deep realization, yet not have that accompanied by any kind of moving experience.

Another aspect of realization is that it is non-reversible, meaning that if one has attained any kind of realization, whether it is only a small glimpse into one's natural state or the realization of intrinsic awareness, then one has realized that. It is not possible for an individual to lose genuine realization. If it could be lost, then obviously one has not realized whatever it is one thought one had realized. To use a very mundane example, if we find out that putting our finger in the fire is not a good idea, then that knowledge stays with us and we won't do it again.

The three different kinds of meditative experiences

Experiences and realizations are *nyam*[56] and *tokpa*[57] in Tibetan. Three different kinds of nyam or meditative experiences are spoken of:

- meditative experience of bliss
- meditative experience of clarity or luminosity
- meditative experience of non-conceptuality

While we do, of course, have many different kinds of experiences, positive experiences are grouped under these three headings. We have experiences that are predominantly blissful, those that have more to do with some kind of clarity or sharpness of the mind, or experiences where our thoughts have slowed and the mind has become very still, which is described as meditative experience of non-conceptuality.

Understanding bliss

With the experience of bliss, we make a distinction between the physical aspect of bliss and its mental aspect. Physically, we may have all kinds of strongly pleasurable sensations. Mentally, we can experience feelings of being uplifted or of joy. We may also start to have other positive experiences such as thinking that we are making progress with our meditation. It is also said that the meditative experience of bliss may manifest in other ways, such as having the desire to laugh for no reason, or wanting to leap about with joy.

As is mentioned in the literature, the experience of bliss, if not handled properly, may also have a downside, as is normally the case. Sometimes when our mood goes up and we are very happy, even ecstatic, this may be followed by dark periods where we feel down or depressed. The idea is that one should not attach too much importance to these things, no matter what is happening.

Actually, the dark or low moments that follow the peak ones are seen, if you like, as the other side of being blissful, being joyous, or ecstatic. They are also seen as symptoms of blissful experience because these high and low experiences often go together. The instruction given to meditators is not to attach too much importance to these experiences, not to take either the high moments or the low moments too seriously, and just have a general, positive attitude towards both.

Often what happens is that a strong sense of attachment and loss comes into the picture after one has some experience of physical and mental bliss. When good experiences come up, we should not become too attached to them because if we do, the feeling of loss is much stronger when they diminish or disappear. With too much attachment to good experiences, we can even interpret reaching a plateau or lull in our meditation as a bad sign. We may feel we have hit a blockade on our road to progress and realization of Mahamudra, as if it is an obstacle course to negotiate.

If we are following Mahamudra meditation, we should not be thinking our experiences should always be positive. "Positive" means positive only from our egocentric point of view that says, "Oh, I find this pleasurable, so I have to have it," or "I have to make sure that it doesn't go away," whereby we want to make some kind of claim on it. The more we think like that, the less control we have over our experiences. Therefore the feelings of attachment and loss become intensified and so our meditation becomes much more difficult to do.

What this also means is that when we have strong attachment and feelings of loss, we rob ourselves of the opportunity to have more meditative experiences. The attachment and feeling of loss and pain that goes with these experiences, and even the blissful experiences that produce these attachments in the first place, all prevent authentic meditative experiences from unfolding and working their way through, so to speak.

The experiences take their course and then come to an end. The proper attitude then lies neither in trying to reduce the sense of attachment and craving for blissful experiences nor trying to reduce the aversion to what we regard from our egoistic point of view to be a negative experience. Instead we try to see these negative experiences in a positive way, as the other side of blissful experience. This is very important.

Understanding clarity

The next one is the experience of clarity, *ösel*[58] in Tibetan. This experience can also have a physical basis in terms of our sensory apparatus. Through having an experience of clarity or luminosity, we can actually sometimes have heightened senses. When we are looking at things, they might become a little more vivid; we may see them in much more detail, as vibrant and almost shimmering. We may hear sound with crispness, as our ability to focus on the incoming sound is heightened.

It is also said we may have quasi-sensory experiences, meaning that even if we have our eyes closed, we might "see" things such as certain colors and shapes. This does not refer to something like an after-image that anybody can see, but is more like having the feeling that we are actually seeing things in the way we normally do. It is not like recalling an object, or imagining something, but spontaneously we may think we are seeing shapes and colors and also hearing all kinds of sounds. There might also be a general heightened sense of clarity, a crisp quality to the mind's own clarity. Even our ability to see things in relation to our thoughts, emotions, and feelings is heightened.

Here, we should have the same attitude: understanding that these experiences do not remain consistently. You might call them episodic, as they arise but don't last, and that is again to be expected. Without wanting to repeat that experience, thinking, "Oh, that was such a great experience. It was so good when I saw things with that sharp level of sensory penetration," we just deal with it and don't get too attached to these things. It is also mentioned in the literature that in general our experience of phenomena is greatly enhanced. These are normally positive experiences and it is a good thing to have such experiences, but we should not get too attached to them. Conversely, when they disappear, we should not get too disappointed and feel the loss intensely.

Understanding non-conceptuality

The third one is the experience of non-conceptuality. "Non-conceptuality" here means we feel there are fewer thoughts going through our mind and our mind becomes more spacious. Not only is the mind more calm and tranquil but there is a feeling of unobstructedness, that the mind is expansive and unbounded. This kind of feeling is, of course, a positive sign; it is a good thing. It is suggested, though, that we should try to see that mind as being a quality of the nature of the mind itself. We can then think that it is a positive thing but, again, not become too attached to it. When other thoughts crop up, we don't then think that we have lost this sense of spaciousness, this ability to remain non-distracted.

We should try to work with all three experiences and, if we work with them, then gradually they will lead us to realization. When we have authentic realization, then of course we may still have *experiences* of bliss, clarity, and non-conceptuality, but we will also have *realization* of bliss, luminosity, and non-conceptuality.

Then, even when we are not actually feeling ecstatic or joyous, no matter what is happening there is still an underlying sense of bliss; some sense of well-being is present, no matter what is going through our minds.

With respect to mental clarity, luminosity, even if there are emotions and discursive thoughts arising, we can maintain a sense of mental clarity, and with our senses we are able to maintain a sense of vividness—or at least do so a bit more consistently.

Non-conceptuality also becomes more stable so that our ability to experience letting go with discursive thoughts is more established. Thoughts and so on then become self-liberated and, from that, one has the experience of non-conceptuality. Even if thoughts arise and emotions arise, one is still able to maintain a sense of non-conceptuality.

Straying

If we have the right kind of approach to dealing with these experiences, we will begin to gain insight into these things. Through gaining insight into bliss, luminosity, and non-conceptuality these become firmly established. They are then a feature of our psychological make-up or way of being.

But, if not, it is said that instead of furthering our meditation with these experiences we may end up stuck, due to attachment, due to feelings of loss. We get attached to the good feelings and then always try to recreate them, chase after them, without realizing that these experiences will come again. Chasing after them, missing them, craving for them actually prevent further experiences from arising. We may want to make them happen, create them, but these experiences have to arise spontaneously so that at the appropriate time and place the experiences will reappear. If one has such experiences, one should feel good about having had them but, at the same time, not develop attachment to them.

It is said in the teachings that if we do not deal with this properly, our experiences of bliss will actually arouse even stronger emotions which will make our meditation very difficult. With mental clarity also, if we do not handle these experiences properly and instead crave for or miss them, then our agitation will increase and our discursive thoughts will become more disturbing. Again, this will cause problems with our meditation. In any case, the thought of loss causes distraction.

Having an open mind towards our experiences and thinking they are all transient so will come and go, is the first approach to take in dealing with meditative experiences. Secondly, even if we do experience the downside of a positive experience, we do not indulge in thinking of it as such but understand it is our dualistic mind telling us that is the case. If we think in that way, positive experiences and all forms of experiences will continue to arise; otherwise we are only going to inflame our emotions and, in doing so, negative feelings about the practice and about meditation experiences will increase.

It is the same with non-conceptuality. If we do not deal properly with the meditative experience of non-conceptuality, we could end up in what we call a state of absorption, and in Mahamudra language that is a bad thing. Even though in other contexts that kind of meditative absorption is sought after, in Mahamudra it is not considered a good experience. It is not a good state to be in because we have to be alert, we have to be aware, we have to be attentive, observant—all of those things. If we are in a sort of lulled, trance-like state, we don't have mental clarity, we are not alert, attentive, and so on, and in the long run that is not beneficial. Therefore one tries not to deliberately cultivate that state of non-conceptuality. If thoughts slow down that is fine, that is great; if they don't slow down, we don't get upset.

By dealing with our experiences in that way, we begin to utilize them to strengthen our meditation and lead us to realization so that all three aspects of our experience become unified. All three aspects—bliss, luminosity, and non-conceptuality—have to be present in our practice, in our mind. We are then not just pursuing bliss or pursuing clarity or non-conceptuality. Sometimes we might think, "Oh, I really love that blissful feeling," or, "When my mind is clear and sharp, resilient, on the mark, I like that." When the mind is so quick, we may want that, and not care so much about bliss. At other times one might think, "There is nothing like the space where my thoughts have practically disappeared and I feel a sense of complete quietude and stillness."

Meditative experiences need to have an element of each of the three aspects. Even though sometimes the meditative experience is more blissful than at other times or the aspect of clarity is greater, nevertheless, at least from one's own side, one should try to think of them as working collectively, not working against or independently of each other. Working collectively, they produce the kind of meditative experience that we need to bring about realization.

The four stages of realization in Mahamudra

Fruition Mahamudra is cultivated in that way and the point is to learn to deal with one's meditative experiences to deepen one's realization. If we deal with these experiences properly, then we will be able to experience:

1. meditative one-pointedness
2. non-conceptuality,
3. one-taste, and
4. non-meditation

These are stages that are described in Mahamudra. When bliss, clarity, and non-conceptuality are all working in unison, the mind is able to gather its strength. Normally our confused mind is dispersed, our mental energy gets scattered. When we are able to practice properly, the mental energies are all drawn inwards, so to speak. Although this is just a figure of speech, the mental energies are brought in and so this is called "one-pointedness" in Mahamudra.

"One-pointedness" does not mean one is only concentrating on one thing. In this context it means the mind is not dispersed. Thus, even if one has these different experiences, for instance, of bliss, clarity, and non-conceptuality, one's mind is not scattered, and that is one-pointedness. If there is one-pointedness, then the mind is not disturbed; thoughts, emotions, feelings can come and go, come and go, with no disturbance. Authentic "non-conceptuality" is then realized and not just experienced.

That leads to "one-taste" where one begins to see that everything has the same flavor, the flavor of emptiness. This refers to everything, including samsara and nirvana. As is often said in the Mahayana and Mahamudra teachings, "There is no difference between samsara and nirvana." Of course it doesn't mean samsara and nirvana are the same but they are the same insofar as they have the same taste, the taste of reality. They are imbued with the same taste or same flavor. When one realizes that and one is not caught up in dualistic notions, then one attains or realizes what is called the stage of "non-meditation."

"Non-meditation," of course, doesn't mean no meditation; non-meditation means *not having to meditate*. One doesn't do formal meditation because everything becomes meditative. Normally, we speak about meditation and post-meditation, and what we experience during meditation differs from what we experience in post-meditation because meditation is always stronger than post-meditation.[59] Even if we can deal with things during meditation, we find it more difficult in post-meditation. For example, after having been meditating for quite a long time, when anger arises during meditation, we may have found a way to deal with it, but in post-meditation situations we may still find it harder to do so. At the stage of non-meditation, though, there is no difference.

This is because one is always attentive, always observant, always aware; one is always in touch with what is going on and one has continuous presence of mind. Therefore, there is no rupture or gap between meditation and post-meditation and so this stage is called the stage of non-meditation. These are the stages of meditation that one goes through until one reaches Mahamudrahood. When one has reached the end stage of non-meditation, one has attained Mahamudra.

KING DOHA
Saraha's Advice to a King

Having gained an understanding of Mahamudra and how it is practiced, we will now look at the *King Doha*. Though he wrote many dohas[60], Saraha wrote three principal ones: the *King Doha*, the *People Doha* (a title also translated as *Doha of the Subject*), and the *Queen Doha*.[61] The *King Doha* is very well organized, so lends itself to being rich study material for this type of meditation. Although we will be studying it in some detail, it is not meant to be taken as an exercise in refining our intellect. In saying that, however, there is quite a bit of analysis involved. The most appropriate approach to have towards the text is to see it as documentation of and on meditative experience. Saraha is in fact talking about his own meditative experience, not simply describing this or that form of practice or meditative experience from a detached point of view. It is thus a personal account of a tantric practitioner—a Mahamudra master describing the paths and stages involved in this form of meditation.

The title of the text is *dohakosha nama charyagiti*[62] in Sanskrit, and *doha dzö chejawa chöpai lu*[63] in Tibetan. We will work through it verse by verse, presenting a commentary on each of the forty verses as we go along. In terms of the title of the text in Sanskrit, doha means "mystical," *kosha* means "treasury," *charya* means "action"—referring in this context to how one puts the Mahamudra practice into action—and *giti* means "songs."

It is customary to make a supplication to your guru before one writes a text. Saraha makes a supplication to his guru so that all adverse conditions are overcome.[64]

I prostrate to the one who has overcome the power of the maras

According to the teachings there are four different kinds of adverse conditions that a spiritual seeker must overcome. These adverse conditions are also referred to as demons or *maras* (Skt.) and are:

1. The adverse conditions that come from our psychophysical condition. As we embark on the spiritual path, we may suffer from all kinds of physical illness, or experience mental strain or even mental breakdown of sorts. In other words, we may experience mental problems associated with our own mental condition.

2. The adverse conditions coming from conflicting emotions. Because of the stirring up of emotions, such as jealousy, anger, intense lust, and ignorance, our spiritual practice can be disrupted and adversely affected. This is called the demon of emotional conflicts.

3. The adverse conditions that come about due to self centeredness. Our self-centeredness or self-absorption interferes with our spiritual progress.

4. The adverse conditions that emanate from our fear of death.

Saraha's intention in making the supplication to his guru is to request that these adverse conditions not come about, so that spiritual progress will be smooth. As pointed out, the real adverse conditions that have potential to disrupt our spiritual practices do not lie in the environment or in any form of external conditions, but rather in things associated with us, ourselves.

In order to make spiritual progress, we have to realize the nature of our own mind, and to realize the nature of the mind, we need guidance. This is made possible by the kindness of our spiritual guides. Saraha's supplication is made to the guru because the guru has the capacity to introduce practitioners to the innate wisdom already present in themselves.

PART 1

How We Have Gone Astray

Verse 1

> *Whipped by the wind,*
> *Still water becomes waves and rollers,*
> *So the king perceives Saraha—*
> *Unity appearing as diversity.*

Saraha is addressing the song to a king whose name is Mahapala. The verse has two sections. We will discuss the first two lines together and then the second two lines.

We need to realize the nature of our own mind but before we do so, we have to understand how we have gone astray. In other words, we have to understand how we have lost our way before we can find our way back to our original state. How things have gone wrong is explained through the use of three examples, and the first is that of the ocean and its waves.

One way of understanding how we have lost touch with our true condition is by using the image of the ocean as an analogy for our own condition. The ocean itself does not waver; the ocean is still in itself. Due to the ocean's currents and the direction in which the wind is blowing, waves are whipped up from the ocean itself. In some areas the ocean is whipped up by high waves and in others it is disturbed by rollers. In Tibetan, this is *ba* and *lap*.[65] In a similar fashion, our own true condition is never disturbed. Dualistic thinking then is compared to a situation where extreme winds are blowing. These dualistic thoughts give rise to all forms of perceptions, conceptions, and sensations, and are stirred up like the waves and rollers. All manner of things then become apparent. If we look at turbulent waves, though, the nature of these waves is water, as is the nature of the ocean itself. In a similar fashion, the myriad things that the mind fabricates and throws up never waver from our own original state and our own nature of mind. Even though myriads of things of great variety are perceived, in reality they have the same nature. This is so because it is the same mind that is responsible for the multitude of perceptions; they are flavored with one taste.

For the next example, Saraha says to the king, Mahapala, that even though Saraha himself is just one person, he is perceived to be many different people, depending upon circumstances and situations. Saraha was born a Brahman. One cannot become a Brahman through education or training; one is born a Brahman. Although Saraha was born a Brahman and mastered the Vedas, he then converted to Buddhism, entered the Buddhist monastic system, and become a great scholar. He later made the change from practicing as a monk to taking on the role of mahasiddha, earning his living by making arrows. In other words, Saraha appeared as a Brahman to some, a Buddhist monk to others, and an arrowsmith to yet others again.

In speaking to the king, Saraha is pointing out that in reality, whether as Brahman, monk, or mahasiddha, he is the same Saraha, and he draws an analogy with the mind. Although mind is one, it gives rise to many different perceptions. Basically Saraha is saying we see the variety only because the mind makes it so. It depends on what the mind chooses to focus on—what features, qualities, or attributes to pick out. We then think of it as that but at the same time there are other options of seeing the same thing.

This makes the last two lines of the verse a little clearer.

Verse 2:

> *A fool, through squinted eyes*
> *Sees a single lamp as two.*
> *Perceived and perceiver are not separate.*
> *How absurd it is, seeing the mind as two things!*

The first two lines in the verse form the analogy. The second two lines convey the meaning of the analogy and describe how that confusion has been generated.

Saraha is, here, pointing out another way to understand how we have become divorced and gone astray from our true authentic state and so misperceive things. He compares the situation to that of a person who is dull-witted and squeezes their eyes, or rolls their eyes upwards or squints, and then looks at a single lamp. For that person, it will appear that there are two lamps instead of one. If that person is not very bright, he or she may then be fooled into thinking there are actually two lamps instead of one.

Saraha suggests this should be seen as similar to the way in which we perceive things dualistically. Though seeing things in this way is mistaken, we do not realize we are doing it, even when we are practicing or meditating. We need to gain knowledge of the natural state, but continue to be fooled by the mistaken notion that what we are seeking and that which is doing the seeking, are separate. In other words, we don't think of the natural state and the mind that perceives the natural state as being not separate. Under the influence of ignorance, we develop this notion of perceiver and perceived as being distinct and unrelated. By thinking that they are unrelated, we become fixated on the "thingness" of both the perceiver and the perceived. We thus completely concretize or solidify the two.

In the last line of the verse, the word *kyé ma*[66] (Tib.) is an expression of wonderment. It means something like, "Alas, how absurd!" We get so easily fooled into thinking of things in a dualistic fashion. Things do not exist unrelated yet we can't help ourselves from perceiving them the way we do. That is a source of wonderment.

Verse 3:

Though many lamps are lit in the house,
The blind remain in darkness.
Co-emergent wisdom permeates us all—
Close by, yet for fools so far away.

Here, again, first we have the analogy and then the meaning; the first two lines contain the analogy and the second two lines contain the meaning.

The natural state of the mind is co-emergent wisdom and this co-emergent wisdom permeates all. This wisdom is not something that we have to attain but is already in us; the light exists already lit within us. Because we have not understood this, we have come under the influence of ignorance. The analogy used here is that of a blind person in a house with the room fully lit by a lamp, so there is no darkness whatsoever. For a blind person there is no difference; they still live in darkness and will only see darkness.

The house is the natural state and the lamp is the wisdom. Because of the presence of ignorance, the light of wisdom is not appreciated; only the darkness of ignorance is perceived. It is another analogy describing the distorted and degraded state that we inhabit. So far the verses have described how we have come to this point, how we have strayed, by using the three analogies:

a) When the wind blows and still water is turned into moving waves.

b) The ignorant press their eyes and see one lamp as two.

c) Though many lamps are lit throughout the house, those with no eyes to see remain in darkness.

Those examples describe how we have become confused, how we have lost touch with our inner light.

Saraha uses a particular technique as his main method of transmission in this doha. It is called "the pairing of metaphor with the actual meaning." In Tibetan this is called *pé dön,*[67] where *pé* means "metaphor" and *dön,* "actual meaning." Saraha uses the technique of pairing metaphor with actual meaning throughout his verses, but does so in slightly different ways. Sometimes there is compatibility between the metaphor or analogy used and the actual meaning, but in other cases the metaphor and actual meaning are contrasted. Hopefully this will become more apparent shortly. Although this discussion is not intended as a discourse on Indian Buddhist literature, nevertheless, if we keep this in mind in general, it will help us to appreciate the verses more.

PART 2

How We Can Rectify the Situation

Saraha then goes on to describe how we should rediscover the light that dispels the darkness, which is the next step. The next verses, by using analogies involving water, the ocean, appearance, and darkness, explain how wisdom is able to illuminate the darkness which shrouds us.

Verse 4:

> *Diverse waterways become one in the ocean.*
> *A multitude of deceptions are dismantled with a single truth.*
> *With the rising of the sun, in one stroke,*
> *All manner of darkness vanishes.*

We know of many famous rivers, such as the Ganges, or the Brahmaputra and so on—the great rivers of this world. They travel through many different lands and countries but eventually all flow into the sea. Once the rivers have merged with the sea, the taste of fresh water merges with the salty taste of the ocean. What is this supposed to convey? It conveys the meaning of the relationship between ultimate and relative truth.

On the relative level we are presented with a multitude of diverse images, perceptions, appearances. On the ultimate level, this multitude of perceptual appearances is flavored with ultimate truth. So even if we are deceived time and time again by apparently diverse appearances, if we are able to gain insight into ultimate truth, then, with one stroke, all the false perceptions become instantly dismantled, as in the next analogy involving the sun and darkness.

During the night, when darkness pervades every direction around us, we need to find some way of illuminating our own little space. We need a means to do this, such as lighting a lamp. We may even have to rely on the small amount of illumination provided by the moon. The next morning, when the sun rises, with one stroke everything becomes illuminated. Then we no longer need to rely on a small source of light to be able to find our way around.

In a similar fashion, by gaining insight into the nature of things, that in itself is sufficient to reveal everything to the practitioner. At that point, one does not need to rely on a little bit of accumulated insight gained through one's practices. These little flashes of insight that one may have gained through one's meditational practices are comparable to relying on small sources of light, like the lighting of candles and lamps in the darkness. If the sun rises, then all sources of light are overshadowed by that light. This then is how we can overcome the condition that we find ourselves in, as described in the first three verses. The basic point of this verse is that we do not need to focus on many separate things. If instead we come into possession of the key point, then everything becomes open and accessible.

The next verse follows on from the previous one, making a similar point in terms of how we can dispel the darkness and find peace even if we are currently tossed around in the turbulent waters of the samsaric ocean.

Verse 5:

> *The ocean, giving rise to rain-bearing clouds,*
> *Receives the water, once again.*
> *Yet, as with unchanging space,*
> *Neither increase nor decrease occurs.*

This may not be a scientific description, but nonetheless we can appreciate the point being made.

Saraha says the ocean does not increase or decrease but, rather, the volume of water in the ocean remains the same. What one can capture in a bucket is not the same as the water in the ocean. If one leaves a bucket out in the open when it rains, the bucket will overflow. When there is no rain and it is left out, then the water evaporates and the bucket becomes empty. Now the ocean, on the other hand, neither increases nor decreases. That is Saraha's point. That is the analogy.

In the summer, due to heat, the vapor from the ocean rises upwards and then the warm air rising into the atmosphere creates clouds. After some time, the clouds begin to produce torrential rain which falls back down into the ocean and onto the dry lands as well. Then all the rivers begin to overflow. There may even be flooding in some areas. All these waters then head back to the ocean. After the monsoon rains have occurred and the water has flowed back to the ocean, although the dams and lakes have changed, there is no such change in the ocean.

Saraha is saying that the ocean is no fuller than it was prior to the monsoon period. Even though the rivers begin to overflow and the lakes are replenished, the ocean itself has not undergone any change, it has not expanded. Conversely, when it does not rain at all, unlike the rivers and lakes on land, the ocean does not then evaporate, but remains constant. Similarly, as human beings we go through many fluctuations.

The analogy above then has to be matched with the next verse which carries the actual meaning of the previous verse.

Verse 6:

Our authentic nature—
Innate and inseparable from the aspects of buddha's being,

Despite our fluctuations as migrators,
Neither is nor is not a substance.

In the same way, we, as sentient beings, go through many different forms of transformation. Sometimes we gain and sometimes we lose, not only in terms of material things and possessions or in terms of our reputation, but also with our own experiences. Sometimes our experiences are positive and reassuring and at other times they are troubling and bring on anxiety, fear, and insecurity. There is constant motion, constant turbulence, but despite all of that, in ourselves, in our authentic state, there is neither increase nor decrease.

When we are faring well, when we are flourishing, there is no increase in our genuine authentic state. When we are feeling miserable or despairing, and feeling hopelessly inadequate, we are not diminished in any way whatsoever in terms of our genuine authentic state of being. This is so because our genuine authentic state is not separable from the being of a buddha. The five aspects of buddha's being are already present within us. They are not something to be acquired with a great deal of effort or through other means, but are there to be rediscovered and retrieved from the depths of our own being.

Therefore, to become enlightened, or to overcome the darkness of ignorance, does not mean we need to find this light from somewhere else. It also does not mean there is only a small flickering, unstable kind of light that, while being there, is under constant threat of being snuffed out. Instead, the light of wisdom that is already innately present is full-blown.

This light neither increases through external signs of development, nor diminishes in relation to what is going on with our different mental states and processes. This innate light is something we are born with and also die with. Because we have this innate light which neither increases nor diminishes, even when we are like the blind person living in the dark house with the lights around but not able to see, still the light is there to be discovered. Even when we are being tossed around on the oceans of samsara with waves of conflicting emotions, still we are not lost. We are still anchored to that source of our own being which is unwavering. That is the meaning of the previous verse. This innate nature, this authentic state, is to be experienced as our own being, not formulated conceptually as a substance or non-substance.

The first three verses explained how we have wandered off from our original dwelling place, so to speak. The next three describe how it is possible to rectify that situation, how we can restore our original state.

PART 3

Preparing to Restore Our Natural State—Overcoming Fixation

We now come to a description of the actual practice, and the instructions on how to follow and attain fruition of the path, at the end, realizing Mahamudra.

Next are four analogies incongruent with the actual meaning, where, as described earlier, the analogy and actual meaning are contrasted. The four analogies emphasize the notion of overcoming fixation. Saraha counsels us not only to let go of our fixation on material things, but also our fixation on things spiritual, unlike the advice found in most traditional Buddhist literature. He emphasizes this time and again in the next few verses.

Verse 7:

> *Forsaking genuine bliss to walk other paths,*
> *Placing hope instead in what is contrived,*
> *Like bees amassing honey but not consuming it,*
> *An opportunity so close is squandered.*

Saraha says that even seasoned practitioners do not really understand how to produce bliss; they do not know the source of bliss. Most spiritual practitioners want to transcend suffering; they want to go beyond pain and are in search of bliss and ecstasy. They are not well-informed however, and so therefore do not know how to go about finding what they desire. Without knowing the source of genuine bliss, they resort to different kinds of spiritual techniques to produce an artificial, temporary bliss. He points out that even if we are using methods that involve various forms of tantric practice such as psychophysical yoga, including special breathing exercises and working with psychophysical energy systems, these will not really produce genuine bliss.

These specific techniques will produce specific forms of pleasure or bliss but this will not be a self-generating kind of bliss. That can come only from *sahaja-jnana*[68] (Skt.). *Sahaja-jnana* means "co-emergent wisdom," which we can access only through the Mahamudra type of meditation. This does not involve using methods, but allows us to naturally enter into a state which has bliss as its natural property. The difference here is of a contrived method versus a non-contrived method of producing bliss. We should try to relinquish our fixation on and attachment to these kinds of temporary pleasures we might gain through the use of different techniques of meditation or yogic practice.

We can see this in three different ways. If we look at bees, bees produce honey which is delicious and has many health properties. But bees, according to Saraha, like to store the honey instead of eating it themselves. So while they are amassing a great quantity of honey, human beings come along and harvest the honey and the bees are left with nothing.

Saraha's point is that if we become attached to the use of different techniques to produce temporary pleasures, we may feel good after doing such practices, but the bliss only lasts a short time. In the meantime, the real bliss generated by *sahaja-jnana* is lost. It is a squandered opportunity, snatched from us. This is the analogy. The bees then are left with having to live on the pollen of flowers which, at least from a human's point of view, is not as delicious as honey. This may perhaps be so from the bees' point of view as well.

The challenge is to learn to differentiate genuine from non-genuine bliss. This is not to say we should abandon the use of these other forms of practice. Saraha was a tantric practitioner himself, but to settle for less when a greater version of something is available is to sell ourselves short. We are mistaken if we fall into this error, and it is something that should be addressed.

Verse 8:

> *Animals don't make suffering for themselves*
> *That's the human expertise.*
> *Rather than drinking the ambrosia of space,*
> *Fixation is what we opt for.*

As animals and humans we all live together on this planet. Although animals' lives are at times violent in terms of how they function and operate, what motivates them for action is immediate; they do not plan or anticipate future moves and consider alternative options in the way human beings do. Human beings are gifted with better mental faculties and better capacity for judgment. Animals, on the other hand, are largely driven by instinct and external stimuli.

But does that mean that human beings act wisely? Not so; in fact, human beings act more foolishly than animals, often because they do not use their faculties to their best advantage. So, instead of finding the lasting peace and happiness they so desperately need and seek, they find further cause for suffering and pain and misery. Saraha's point seems to be that in fact meditation practitioners, those who have embarked on the spiritual path, behave in a very similar fashion to ordinary human beings. Animals are endowed with very limited abilities and capacities yet use them to maximum effect. Ordinary human beings, despite being gifted with greater abilities and capacities, allow themselves to be compromised. Similarly, it is quite possible that yogis and yoginis, instead of trying to look at the essence of things, at what matters most, can become side-tracked. They can be completely engrossed in the details of practices and meditative experiences, trying to refine their conceptual comprehension of the subject-matter. They then forget to actually deal with their own immediate experiences.

So again, we should try to let go of our attachment to these things, our fixation on spiritual matters. The point is that the so-called worldly people come to harm from pursuing sensual pleasures without thinking, without reflecting. They simply act on impulse, and therefore suffer. Similarly, yogis and yoginis also become attached to this or that system of meditation, or this or that theory from such and such philosophical or theological system designed to produce spiritual understanding. In contrast, Mahamudra practitioners need to let go of fixation on wanting to continually refine their conceptual comprehension of things. They need to let go of obsessing over what is to be discarded and what is to be cultivated or improved upon.

This is the second way through which we overcome our attachment and fixation in order to progress on the path. Just as bees and ordinary beings come to harm through unbridled expression of their instinctual desires and impulses, yogis too fall victim to fixation. Although human beings are not the same as other creatures, nevertheless their fixation is their own worst enemy; the one thing they most cherish is the very thing that brings them grief in the end.

Verse 9:

> Spurning sandalwood's fragrant aroma,
> Flies are attracted to excrement.
> Likewise we turn from transcending misery,
> Captivated by habitual negativity.

This verse is quite blunt; it does not require significant commentary. Saraha reflects upon the fact that one does not see great hosts of flies aggregating and settling on pieces of sandalwood even though sandalwood is wonderfully aromatic. Instead, they settle on human excrement and other such foul things. In a similar way, we should not allow ourselves to become accustomed to our negative tendencies.

If we allow ourselves to become accustomed to our negative tendencies, then we will become impervious to change. We need to have real conviction that becoming accustomed to our negative tendencies is a completely mistaken attitude to have. The mistake we are making when we do this lies in thinking that we should put our trust in things that can be lost. In the end, doing so will only bring grief. Instead, we should search for the source of our happiness, the source of meaning and purpose in our life. Thus, on the path, we also have to let go of our fixation on temporary things that do not bring ultimate happiness. According to Saraha, such fixation will bring us to our own ruin.

We now come to the last analogy used to help us understand how to overcome fixation on the path. Saraha's central point is that before we do Mahamudra practice, we first have to fully comprehend the need to let go of fixation. Otherwise, if we prematurely embark on the path, we are bound to get fixated on all kinds of things on the way.

Verse 10:

> *An ox's hoof-print filled with water soon dries out.*
> *It is not so precious.*
> *Though seemingly perfect and stable, experiences,*
> *No matter how desirable, will too evaporate.*

Another fixation a meditation practitioner must be wary of has to do with their own meditative experiences. As soon as one starts to meditate, there will be signs. There might even be apparitions, visions, quasi-visual experiences, and the hearing of things and so forth. A myriad of unusual experiences is possible. Again, in this instance, the meditator should be cautious and wary and not think these unusual experiences are related to some sort of spiritual breakthrough or are a sign of gaining enlightenment. Even if they are good signs, we should not become attached to them; we should not think they are amazing and precious, to be cherished and hung onto tenaciously. Rather, we should recognize that even though they are positive signs and contain positive qualities, these qualities are limited. If we do this, we avoid fixating on what is limited, for this prevents the unlimited from bursting forth into our being.

It is like ignoring a vast lake and becoming fascinated by a relatively miniscule amount of water captured inside some animal's hoof-print. So we should always be open to the unlimited and not become fixated on the limited gains or progress we have made, or the various signs or symbolic indicators. Putting too much stock in them is an important point to keep in mind. The limited gains we make, and the limited qualities we attain, will fluctuate. Sometimes these experiences will be good and remain for some time, but at some point they will vanish and dry up, just like the water captured in a hoof-print. When this happens and they fail to recur, it concerns us greatly, leading to mental agitation.

If we are open to the unlimited and the infinite, we become enriched and full. Again, it is about not settling for imitation and not losing sight of the real thing. Its meaning is akin to the old saying, "all that glitters is not gold."

That concludes the section on what we need to do to prepare ourselves on the meditation path of Mahamudra. We need to avoid getting caught up in unnecessary distractions, as these distractions come largely from our inveterate tendency to become fixated on things.

PART 4

Determining the Significance of the Path

Determining the real significance of the meaning of the path is also explained with the use of four analogies. These are non-contradictory analogies.

Verse 11:

> *Just as sea water evaporating from the ocean*
> *Turns into clouds of sweet rain,*
> *A mind released can benefit others.*
> *What we see as poison becomes ambrosia.*

The first analogy involves sea water, which is salty by nature. Sea water is generally not potable. However, due to changes in temperature, vapor rises into the atmosphere and the saltiness of the salt water is transformed. First it turns into clouds and then the clouds produce rainwater, which is sweet and completely drinkable. So what is drinkable comes from a source which was initially not so. This analogy explains how the mind uses concepts, particularly in relation to our judgments upon what we regard as virtuous or non-virtuous, or beneficial and non-beneficial action.

Generally speaking, a person who has embarked on the spiritual path has to exercise judgment with respect to their actions. A practitioner needs to see whether their actions are beneficial or causing harm. This is extremely important. But if a practitioner does not see through the judgmental mind itself and see the mind which forms these judgments as being empty and non-substantial, then even virtuous thoughts and deeds are binding; they do not lead to ultimate freedom. The practitioner is left still bound to the worldly condition.

Even when we have thoughts of compassion and want to do things that bring a great deal of pleasure to others or provide them with some relief from suffering, if our mind has not been freed into its natural state, whatever thought-formations we may have do not find release into the luminous nature of mind. Thus we do not drink that nectar, and we do not find freedom. If in following this path we are able to release all forms of judgment, all forms of conception, into the natural state of the mind which is by nature luminously clear, then those judgments, those thought-formations in themselves, become self-liberated. It is thus like salt water turning into fresh water. In other words, discursive thoughts and various mental formations become transformed. If they are not transformed, then even positive thought-formations do not lead to complete freedom.

Verse 12:

> The ineffable—this is not suffering.
> Non-meditation—that itself is genuine bliss. Likewise,
> Though the sound of thunder may invoke fear,
> The rain it portends matures crops.

The first verse in this section emphasized the point of not simply being satisfied with converting negative thought-formations into positive ones but attempting to liberate even the positive thought-formations into the natural state of the mind.

In this next verse, using the analogy of the thunderclap, one is encouraged to gain some understanding of ultimate reality. Here, the metaphor is that, as a portending sign of a coming monsoon, a lot of activity gathers in the sky. There are rumblings, thunder, and lightning and so forth which eventually bring rain. Often such activities appear ominous to people, who generally react to them with fear. For example, they may be afraid of being struck by lightning. If one really thinks about it though, the activity in the sky is not a bad sign at all but a good sign, because these rumbling sounds portend rain, which means crops will flourish and then food will be plentiful. So this thunderstorm activity actually needs to be greeted with joy, and not fear and trepidation.

The meaning refers to the need to take care in how we understand the notion of emptiness. Without training, when we first hear of things being empty in nature and non-substantial, we may react with fear. The thought of emptiness may give rise to notions that nothing exists or that nothing really matters any longer, and everything will simply disintegrate and crumble and vanish into thin air. But if we develop a proper understanding of emptiness, then we will soon realize there is no need for that kind of fear and anxiety at all. The notion of emptiness should be greeted with joy rather than fear and trepidation. Just as the monsoon rain brings a bountiful crop for the farmers, similarly, gaining a proper understanding of emptiness leads one to the true experience of bliss, a bliss which is not contrasted with suffering.

Our normal experience of pleasure and happiness is necessarily contrasted with painful experiences, undesirable experiences, but the bliss that issues forth from gaining insight into emptiness is of a different order, a different kind. This form of bliss is an unchanging bliss. We can access unchanging bliss when we learn to be in our natural state without striving. So when we meditate in the Mahamudra style of meditation, we should not try to meditate; meditation should not be something that we need to do. Thus we learn to relinquish all thoughts of meditation as an object, the meditator as a subject, and meditation itself as the act that the meditator performs.

A meditator able to enter into this state is liberated from karmic imprints, sullied or unsullied. Sullied or tainted karmic imprints come from engaging in negative thought-forms and actions. Positive, unsullied karmic imprints ensue from engaging in positive actions. In one's natural state, one is freed from all such imprints. Thus one is able to enjoy true unchanging bliss. This is so because there is no striving in terms of wanting to reduce suffering or produce pleasure, nor effort to avoid acting negatively or to do good things. From that point of view then, the teachings on emptiness should be used to discover one's innate wisdom. They should not be greeted with fear and trepidation but with joy, just like greeting the monsoon rain.

Verse 13:

> *Thusness has neither start nor conclusion.*
> *It has no place of abiding—no beginning, no end, no in-between.*
> *To those befuddled by conceptualization,*
> *Emptiness enmeshed with great compassion is how it's put.*

This verse is about co-emergent wisdom—*lhenchik kyepai yeshé*[69].

Co-emergent wisdom, which is inextricably linked to our natural state, is not something that comes in to being or ceases to exist. We should therefore not think there is any kind of beginning or end to co-emergent wisdom. It is a spontaneously naturally-produced state. In other words, it does not come into being due to causes and conditions. If it were to come about due to causes and conditions, then, without certain causes and conditions being present, it would not have come into existence. If it were dependent on causes and conditions for its perpetual existence, then when those causes and conditions either changed or shifted or ceased to exist, it would go through various forms of change and would itself cease to exist. Co-emergent wisdom therefore cannot be seen as something that has a beginning or an end. It is then not causally produced but is a spontaneously-risen state.

The question is about finding oneself in that state; it is not a question of how it has come about. It is spontaneously present whenever one rests oneself into that state. As a meditator, one should not entertain thoughts of this state as being something that is substantial, tangible, graspable, or amenable to conceptual or verbal formulation. It is inexpressible yet experience-able. When one encounters it, it appears yet it is empty in itself. While appearing it remains empty; while remaining empty it appears.

Co-emergent wisdom should not be thought of as something we can pin down and grasp at, articulate through verbal formulations, or conceptually analyze in a neat and tidy way. It is pointless trying to trace its beginning. Co-emergent wisdom dwells in the place of "no place," so one cannot find the place where it begins and one cannot find the place where it ends. It is totally impartial, so one cannot say it tends towards this or that side of any dimension. In other words, we should resist thinking about co-emergent wisdom as we think about things.

Whenever we think about things, it is in terms of space and time; we think in terms of where something is or when something is taking place. Everything has to be put in some kind of spatiotemporal framework, but here no spatiotemporal framework applies. This is what it meant by "it appears yet it is empty." It appears because we experience it, but it is empty because we cannot use spatiotemporal categories and say it is this or it is that. Nothing definite can be said about it and nothing definite can be conceived about it. We cannot seize it and say this is what co-emergent wisdom is like. Because we are unable to apply spatiotemporal categories to it, it lacks the characteristics of being a thing of some kind. Therefore it is empty. But it is not non-existent, because in and through meditation we can experience it and it appears. This is what is meant by "while appearing it remains empty, while remaining empty it appears." That way it does not then tend towards partiality; it does not tend towards emptiness or appearance.

Co-emergent wisdom is introduced to the meditator in terms of how it appears, how it is experienced in the form of intrinsic awareness, how it is experienced in the form of bliss or meditative ecstasy, and through the illuminating powers of the state. Also, such illuminating experience is not separate from compassion. We should not think of it as a simple case of cognitive transformation. It is not that something happens to our cognitive nature of mind while our emotional, affective side remains untouched. This intrinsic awareness, co-emergent wisdom, is inherently linked to compassion. It is not linked to just any kind of compassion though, but to great compassion, *mahakaruna* (Skt.), *nyingjé chenpo*[70] (Tib.).

Great compassion is also unproduced. Great compassion arises not for this or that reason; it is "self-presencing." A natural out-flowing of compassion occurs, not just because we see someone who has lost a leg or is in a similar difficult situation. It is compassion of a different order in that it is unproduced, uncaused. It is part of the properties, so to speak, of this state. Such a state occurs in the form of the union of emptiness, co-emergent wisdom, and compassion as exemplified by the statement: *tongnyi nyingjé nyingpo chen*[71] (Tib.). This means "emptiness is the essence of compassion" where emptiness and *mahakaruna*, great compassion, are completely integrated, intermeshed, interspersed, conjoined, and experienced with one flavor, *rochik*[72] (Tib.).

Verse 14:

> *Just as bees know*
> *To find nectar in a flower,*
> *So, befuddled fools should fully comprehend*
> *Not casting away the essence of samsara and nirvana.*

This verse deals with the question, "If it is the case that everyone is in possession of co-emergent wisdom, that it is ever-present and no one can either gain or lose it, how is it that some individuals experience it, access it, and yet others are completely oblivious of its presence?"

Again, an analogy involving bees is used to explain how the wise can access the natural state while those who are ignorant remain completely oblivious of it. A comparison is made here with bees and pollen. Only bees know about the nutritional value of pollen and are attracted to flowers. If bees, even though not in the immediate vicinity, get a hint fresh flowers are in the area, they will seek them out to extract the pollen. Other creatures such as tadpoles and frogs may in fact be closer to the flowers than the bees, but are completely oblivious of them.

Similarly, those individuals who are able to access co-emergent wisdom can do so only because they know how. It all depends on whether one has this knowledge or not; it has nothing to do with what is there. It is the same situation as that of creatures other than bees, those that do not take advantage of the flowers. It is not because the flowers are not there, but because they don't know what is available and how to access it. Practitioners of Mahamudra, for instance, are able to access their natural state because they are not searching for nirvanic quietude, on the one hand, nor are they trying to escape from samsaric bondage, on the other. If meditators know how to extract the true essence of things, then they do not need to renounce this or that thing, but are able to realize their ultimate goal, because they are in possession of that secret knowledge.

In this section, we have looked at four verses (verses 11-14). Basically, the last of these says that bees are able to extract the true pollen, an analogy for the knowledge that samsara and nirvana are not opposite poles, that understanding the true essence of *both* leads to liberation. Each of these four verses involves developing a knack. If one has the knack of doing something then, even if it is a very weighty and complicated thing, it can be done very simply and almost effortlessly. That is the basic thrust of these four verses.

The first one talks about how different mental formations and thought-forms can be transformed if we have the knack, just as the salt water of the sea is transformed into the fresh water of rain. Next, if one can really get the knack of understanding the ultimate reality of emptiness, which is inexpressible and beyond conception, then everything becomes revealed. Consequently, if one greets emptiness with as much joy as one greets the monsoon rain, then one becomes liberated. Thirdly, if one develops the knack of understanding that the ultimate state is beyond formulation, in terms of space-time categories, then again one becomes liberated into one's natural state. Finally, if one develops the knack of extracting the essence of samsara and nirvana, one is liberated not by trying to renounce samsara and pursue nirvana, but by understanding the essence of both.

In the four verses that follow, congruent analogies and incongruent analogies are interspersed.

The first analogy starts with verse 15.

Verse 15:

Seeing an image in a mirror
A fool misconstrues what is there.
So we turn from ultimate truth,
Relying instead on what is false.

In this particular verse, Saraha emphasizes the notion that we need not be seduced and bedazzled by the multitude of appearances that we encounter on a daily basis. Appearances, here, refer to the empirical experiences we have of the world, particularly in relation to how things are perceived through our sensory apparatus.

This is illustrated by use of the analogy of a fool looking into a mirror. If someone who has never seen a mirror is suddenly presented with one and is told to look into it and sees a face there, that person does not see their own face. They see the person in the mirror as being somebody else. This may be hard to imagine, but if one did not know what a mirror, was one might be fooled into thinking that it was someone else's face. Or to approach the idea a little differently, if the mirror was presented to a baby or infant, they might not recognize their own face but see the face of another baby.

To use a more modern and risqué example, when Tibetans first escaped from Tibet and went to India, one day a Tibetan nomad walked into a movie theatre and saw everyone sitting there. He sat down and watched the movie and saw a scene set in India. In India, they have public taps positioned all over the place where people can get their water and wash their clothes and bathe themselves. In the scene, a woman comes along and begins to take off her clothes to bathe. The nomad was getting excited over this when a train came along and blocked the view of the woman. He became most upset. He went away and next day came back and, as he was watching the movie, the same scene came on again. At the very moment when the woman began to take off her clothes, the train came along again. The nomad then said, "Why does this train always have to be on time?" He did not realize it was a projection but thought it was real.

Another example could be that of presenting a mirror to a

monkey. The monkey is likely to make faces and growl at the image, thinking of it as another monkey. The core idea is that we get duped by what we perceive, so in the same fashion, on a daily basis, we do not realize we are being fooled by what we see. We project characteristics, attributes, and properties onto the things that we perceive. We then see those properties as belonging to the things themselves, rather than being imputed or foisted upon what we perceive. Just as a fool thinks of the reflected face as belonging to another person, similarly we also see attributes and qualities in things which are not present in the things themselves.

When we don't realize that we are foisting characteristics, attributes, and properties onto the things we perceive with our projections, just like the monkey, we may react to what we perceive with lust or anger or even violence. So the properties we have projected may invoke violence in us. The properties are first projected outwards and then we become angry. Alternatively, if the properties of a thing are attractive to us, they may elicit lustful thoughts. They draw us to that object.

Saraha's basic point in this verse is that we have to realize that, and not get so easily worked up, thinking of all these things coming at us, without realizing our own responsibility and participation in our experiencing of them. We usually see things as impinging on us and coming at us, forcing us to react. On the contrary, according to Saraha and many others, it is we who are acting on things. Then, in our deluded fashion, we act towards them as if we ourselves have no role to play in the experiences we endure at any given time.

The next verse uses the example of a fragrant flower, showing meditative concentration to be continuous when one has realized the wheel of the three kayas.

Verse 16:

> *A flower's fragrance has no form*
> *Yet reaches far and wide.*
> *So, through the nature that is formless,*
> *The wheels of the mandala will be known.*

In this particular verse, Saraha emphasizes that even if we meditate and try to realize how creatively our mind is operating and giving structure and form to our sensory experiences, the appearances of sense objects will not disappear, but will continue to arise.

As pointed out in the previous verse, we are normally deceived by appearances, but just because appearances arise continuously, it does not necessarily mean we need be deceived by them. While appearances arise, we can simply remain in an uncontrived, natural state. This uncontrived, natural state does not lead to the occurrence of distorted forms of perceptions and conceptions with respect to our experiences of things. In this way, we can still maintain a continuous state of contemplation, of equilibrium.

If we maintain this state, then everything we experience can be seen as the workings of the wheels of the three kayas or three aspects of a buddha's being: the physical aspect; the communicative aspect which is related to speech; and the continuous manifestation of the authentic state of being. The physical aspect of a buddha's being is *nirmanakaya*[73] (Skt.), the communicative aspect of a buddha's being is *sambhogakaya*[74] (Skt.), and the authentic aspect of a buddha's being is *dharmakaya*[75] (Skt.).

The impure perceptions we are subject to in our deluded state then become pure perception. This is so if and when we are able to maintain our natural state, when we are able to perceive everything we experience as the workings of the wheel of the three kayas. In other words, we are able to perceive everything we experience as manifestations of enlightened, non-deluded perceptions.

The illustration of this is the flower and its fragrance. The beauty of a flower is visible to the naked eye but its fragrance, on the other hand, is not. It has no form, no color, no shape, and yet the fragrance reaches far and wide. Even if the flower itself is not immediately perceived, the fragrance reaches the nasal organ and one can immediately smell it. Similarly, if one maintains one's natural state of being, then the full effect of the workings of the three kayas will be manifest, although they may not be perceptible. How they work is intangible, not graspable, but nonetheless one can experience it. The workings of the three kayas are intimated in the most subtle and varied ways.

Basically, to be in the natural state means being in a state where the meditator, while doing meditation, is not concerned about whether he or she is meditating or not meditating. Being without all kinds of conceptual proliferation of even thoughts of meditation or non-meditation is genuine *samadhi*[76] (Skt.); that is the genuine way to rest in one's natural state. If we are in that state, then everything we experience as a meditator, both internally and externally will be seen as stirrings of the three aspects of a buddha's being.

The next verse shows, through the example of ice, how concepts are concretized into something hard and dense.

Verse 17:

When icy winds gust over water,
What was fluid becomes like stone.
So, with our distorted beliefs,
We fools solidify the formless.

This analogy illustrates how our mind becomes inflexible, rigid. In the summer, water is a fluid we can pour into any container and drink yet in winter, water freezes and becomes ice. When it freezes, one can use it as a hard object or even make a sculpture from it, a sculpture as solid as rock.

In a similar fashion, the mind in its nature is fluid, malleable, pliant, and buoyant but, due to bad habits, the mind can become very entrenched and set in its own ways. These habitual patterns become solidified. Various mental states and processes become ingrained. The mind then becomes very rigid and unworkable.

So in winter when cold winds blow very hard and the temperature drops, waterways become completely frozen over. Similarly, through movement and turbulent activities such as the upsurge of emotional conflicts, which are likened to the blowing gusts of wind, mental habits are created which then become solidified. The mind becomes completely non-pliant, lacks buoyancy, and is heavy, solid, and inflexible. The solidification is helped along by greater and greater fixation on things and by feelings of certainty, the certainty of seeing what one considers to be true as being so without question, without doubt.

Doubt plays an important part in the practice. According to Buddhism, we fail to doubt the things we, in fact, should doubt. On the other hand, we doubt things we should not be so skeptical about. We think "seeing is believing" and that anything beyond that is something to be suspicious of. Again, Saraha is addressing how this occurs, how we take everything we experience to be so real. Because our habits are so ingrained, so well-entrenched, it is almost as if we are pre-programmed to see things in this way. Fortunately, this process is reversible. Just as blocks of ice can melt, similarly a mind resistant to change and transformation can yield to spiritual practices and thus become less fixated and more amenable and pliant.

The next verse is the fourth example in this group of verses where, through the analogy of a jewel in a morass, it is shown that the mind itself is not affected by stains:

Verse 18:

Though mired in samsaric bondage and nirvanic freedom,
Our natural state remains untouched.
Submerged in mud, a precious gem's lustre,
Whilst not evident, does not diminish.

The mind itself has two aspects. It is endowed with two-fold purity: the mind's intrinsic purity and its potential for purification. This is called *dakpa nyiden*[77] in Tibetan. This means that the mind by nature is pure and, in addition to that, it has the potential to be purified of the so-called adventitious defilements. Thus the defilements are not intrinsic to the nature of the mind and are therefore removable. Their scope for removability is what is called the potential for purification.

In Tibetan also, in *Gyu Lama, Mahayana Uttaratantra*[78] (Skt.), it says: *rangzhin namdak*[79] and *lobur draldak*.[80] *Rangzhin namdak* means that mind is pure, that buddha-nature is pure, in itself. It does not become pure because one has done something to make it pure, but it is pure by nature. *Lobur draldak* means that it becomes pure once the adventitious defilements have been lifted. In other words, even if the nature of the mind is pure, we are not aware of it. So that state of non-awareness has to lift, and once it has lifted, we see our original purity.

Our experiences both of samsaric bondage and nirvanic freedom have their origin in the natural state of our being. This particular condition is illustrated by the example of a jewel encased in mud. If a precious stone or jewel drops into a swamp, then it will disappear, become submerged. The radiant brilliance, though, the iridescent, glowing nature of the jewel or stone is not diminished. The mud has no effect; it does not penetrate the jewel. If for example you throw something else such as a piece of copper or iron into the mud, then, gradually, over a period of time, it rusts or corrodes until eventually it disappears in the swamp. A precious stone or diamond dropped into the swamp, though, will not be penetrated and therefore its glowing and iridescent nature will not diminish. Similarly, the mind's original brilliance remains, despite its being encased in the pollutant layers of defilement.

Firstly, Saraha discusses the way we are dazzled by appearances. Then he turns to how we are able to maintain our own natural state even while immersed in such appearances. After that, he discusses the actual origin of this fixation: where it comes from; how our mind becomes rigid; why fixation develops. Finally, Saraha points out that even though all these things happen, our original state remains unaltered, unchanged. This, therefore, is the foundation upon which our practice has to be erected—on the knowledge that our own natural state is untarnished, immaculate, and completely untainted by adventitious defilements.

Next, through the use of two opposing or incongruent analogies, the co-dependent arising of cause and effect is shown. This section has two divisions. In Tibetan, *pé*[81] is the word translated as "example" or "analogy."

Verse 19:

> *When ignorance flares up, wisdom dies down.*
> *When ignorance flares up, suffering flares up.*
> *From a seed, a seedling sprouts;*
> *From the seedling, foliage forms.*

Saraha's point here is quite simple. We may come up with all kinds of theories about what ignorance is and what wisdom is and so forth but, according to Saraha, we can greatly simplify this by looking at what perpetuates ignorance and what increases wisdom. Our ignorance is fanned by discursive thoughts. As discursive thoughts begin to proliferate, our mind becomes dimmer, and when the discursive thoughts become more settled and less active, then the mind begins to show more clarity. One's ability to think and see things clearly then increases proportionately. Ignorance and wisdom are thus opposed. When there is ignorance, there is no capacity for wisdom to shine forth. When there is wisdom, there is a definite decrease in terms of ignorance. Therefore the best way to address this situation is to deal with our discursive thoughts. If ignorance increases when our disturbing thoughts are most active and at their highest level, then obviously, if we deal directly with them, our mind should become clearer and more lucid. If our mind becomes more clear and lucid, wisdom has already become manifest.

Saraha's point seems to be that we need not speculate over the nature of wisdom or ignorance, asking questions like: "How should we define ignorance?" or "How should we define wisdom?" Rather, through pure observation in terms of our own experience in meditation, we can come to appreciate the fundamental point. Discursive thoughts agitate the mind and the agitated mind then becomes blind. Conversely, as agitation decreases when the mind is less disturbed by discursive thoughts, clarity resurfaces and the mind's ability to clearly see things naturally presents itself.

This process is illustrated by the analogy of the seedling and a tree and branches. If there is a seedling, then branches will appear, and if there is no seedling, then branches will not appear. If there is a seed, that seed will germinate and become a seedling and then grow into a shrub. Then from that will grow branches and foliage and so forth. In a similar fashion, we have the seed of ignorance and the seed of wisdom. Discursive thoughts fan the seed of ignorance prompting all kinds of defilements to proliferate. The converse happens when the discursive thoughts decrease; the seed of wisdom increases and so wisdom begins to flower and flourish.

Verse 20:

> *By analyzing, through the reasoning of neither one nor many,*
> *Abandoning clarity,*
> *One gazes into the pit of nihilism and heads for the lower realms.*
> *Who could be more deserving of compassion?*

Here, Saraha is critiquing the conventional vipashyana type of meditation, particularly the type based on Nagarjuna and Chandrakirti's Madhyamaka logic, or the Prasangika-Madhyamaka logic, of *reductio ad absurdum* (Latin). One of the forms of reasoning used is that of one or many. It is called *chikdu dralgyi tentsik*[82] in Tibetan.

With this approach, one selects a random object and tries to determine if one can see it as being one or many. For example, a selected substance such as wood has many attributes, such as being of a certain color, shape, and so forth. Through such reasoning one comes to the conclusion that it is neither one nor many, nor both nor either. One can't hold any position in terms of the tetralemma. It is more common to talk in terms of a dilemma, but we can also have a trilemma, or as in this case, a tetralemma. If we say something exists or does not exist, that is a dilemma. Through the use of this *reductio ad absurdum* reasoning one realizes that one cannot subscribe or adhere to any of the approaches of the so-called "four-cornered logic" of the tetralemma. Finally one comes to realize things have no inherent existence because (i) they do not exist, (ii) they do not, not exist, (iii) they do not both exist and not exist, and finally, (iv) they neither exist nor not exist. That is the tetralemma. Most people would probably give up and say, "Yes, I'm convinced, please spare me the logic, I concede!" The objective, though, is to undertake the long process of reasoning in order to conclude that things are empty of inherent existence.

Saraha, however, suggests the meditator need not be overly

concerned with the use of logic and reasoning in this fashion. Of course, these approaches have their uses, but they are not the most important methods by which to understand the nature of the mind. What the meditator really needs to know is that if one thinks of the mind as having some kind of substance, then one falls into the extreme of eternalism, or what we might call substantialism. If we think like this, we may believe there is something called the mind which we can get hold of, pin down, and clearly define. On the other hand, if we say the mind is free of that and there is nothing, then we fall into the opposite extreme, the nihilistic extreme. And, as Saraha says, if we fall into this extreme, then we will plunge into the lower realms.

In meditation, when we start to look for the mind, we cannot find the mind; we cannot simply say about the mind, "There it is." That reveals the mind is empty. Yet when we look into it, it is not mere nothingness; there is mental clarity. There is something which is illuminating. Thus it is not non-existent.

A meditator has to be very careful, according to Saraha, so as to not fall into the nihilistic pit. He seems to be warning us that using the Madhyamaka logic to extreme lengths could quite possibly lead us into the nihilistic pit, because we would see everything as empty. We would analyze agent and action and they would be revealed to be empty, and therefore karmic cause and effect too would be revealed to be empty. Similarly, we analyze the samsaric condition and nirvanic condition and both are revealed to be empty, and so on and so forth. In this way we may be driven unwittingly into the extreme nihilist position. Saraha says this kind of meditator is pitiable and, as they are mistaken in their efforts, should be an object of our compassion. By analyzing and analyzing excessively, we could be led to the pit of nihilism and so must be alert to its dangers.

Saraha is not denying the value of analytical meditation. There are two different kinds of meditation: *chegom*[83] and *jogom*,[84] meditation of contemplation and meditation of analysis, or contemplative meditation and analytical meditation. In Buddhism, even philosophical analyses like these are seen as meditation because they encourage a meditative way of thinking. Saraha's point is that if one does it too much, then one could fall into the nihilistic pit, which would be a pitiable, sorry sight.

PART 5

Discarding Attachments to Mistaken Paths

Next is the main section of the description related to Path Mahamudra, *lam chakgya chenpo*[85] which involves discarding attachments to mistaken paths.

Before discussing the Mahamudra path, Saraha lists some alternative spiritual paths one can follow with Buddhism and then explains why they are in some way inadequate. He is not suggesting they are incorrect in themselves but that, if followed incorrectly, they will fail to deliver the real thing. In other words, by following them incorrectly, one will only end up with a semblance of spiritual realization; one will not attain genuine realization. Saraha seems to indicate that following other paths will involve more elaborate rituals and more complicated practices, therefore giving more room to the possibility of going astray. The Mahamudra path is presented as being simpler, thereby allowing less room for getting sidetracked.

The first path that he criticizes is the Tantric practice of *karmamudra*[86] (Skt.), which in the West is known as sexual yoga, *lekyi chakgya*[87] in Tibetan.

Verse 21:

> *Fools, obsessed with sexual embrace,*
> *Declare the ultimate to be known—*

> *Like wandering to others' doorsteps*
> *Telling lewd tales of Kamarupa.*

Saraha's point is that we should really try to look for the great bliss that practices such as Mahamudra afford us and not get attached to practices such as karmamudra. Attachment to the bliss of karmamudra that comes from sexual congress is not comparable to the genuine bliss that can arise from within. The first is called "sullied bliss" and the other, that arising from within one's own being, is the bliss which is unchanging and ultimate.

Some people who follow the tantric path think that by engaging in karmamudra they experience unchanging, ultimate bliss. In doing so, they mistake what is actually more base for what is higher. Saraha compares this to the story of Kamarupa. *Kama rupa*[88] (Skt.) basically means "sensual form." *Kama*—not "karma"—means sensuality and *rupa* means form.

Saraha suggests it is like somebody who has had little sexual success going around asking, "Where is Kamarupa?" In telling that story properly we should imagine a wealthy person who has everything and yet leaves home to wander all over the place. Finally, in a desolate, godforsaken place, they wander around and stand in front of the doors of people's homes talking about Kamarupa and telling lewd sexual stories. Such a person is only talking about kama rupa, though. This is a play on words. Kamarupa is the name of a woman but, at the same time, it means sensual form. So kama rupa could be anyone; it could be a man for a woman, a woman for a woman, or anyone to whom one is attracted. His point is: "Why not try to tap into the natural great bliss that we can find within ourselves? Why not put energy into that, instead of trying to seek bliss outside ourselves through the means of kama rupa?" He is not necessarily suggesting that these tantric practices are wrong but that if we do not fully understand what we are doing, then we can get trapped. If we are trapped, we cannot progress further.

That is one tantric path he cautions against, or at least suggests we should be wary of, in the sense of avoiding fixation on the bliss that is produced.

The next Tantric practice he cautions against is the practice of *pranayama*[89] (Skt.).

Verse 22:

> *Generating winds in the empty house, descent from*
>   *the essence of space—*
> *So many ways are contrived.*
> *Practicing wrongly, tormenting themselves,*
> *All the yogis do is faint.*

Saraha discusses these practices from his own experience. He has done them all himself. Many tantric practitioners utilize the body as a means of attaining the different levels of rarefied states of consciousness. They do this by working with psychophysical energy, the psychophysical energy pathways, and life-essence; *prana*, *nadi*, and *bindu*[90] (Skt.).

Again, one must understand that, by and large, whatever results we may get, what we experience remains within the realm of sullied spiritual experience. In addition to that, it is a contrived method, not the natural method of Mahamudra. This is so because the practitioner has to put themselves into many difficult physical postures and activate unusual breathing exercises, et cetera.

One of the methods used in Tantrism is to visualize one's body as empty inside so we can then scoop up the pranic energy and fill our body with that energy. There is also the shooting out of pranic breath, like an arrow, turning it around in the system like a wheel, or holding the pranic breath as if it were contained in a vase. Then there are methods of visualizing a seed symbol such as *ham* in the crown chakra or crown psychophysical energy center, where the life-essence (bindu) begins to melt. This produces many extremely pleasurable sensations as it travels through the energy centers.

These "contrived" tantric methods all produce different results. Sometimes these practices, if not done properly, lead the practitioner to become very attached to them. Done to such an extreme level, one may very well become ill. Some may lose consciousness; they may faint because of improper breathing or excessive effort. They can become obsessed, like a body-builder working out 24 hours a day. One can find body-builders like that in the gym; they even regret going to sleep because they would rather be working-out.

Again, when engaging with this kind of practice, one should not think it is the ultimate, the "be all and end all" of practice. Of course, these practices have their place and they can and should be done if one is a tantric practitioner with the requirements and authorizations to engage in them. Even if one has the authorizations, the necessary empowerments and *abhishekas*[91] (Skt.) to undertake such practices, one must still exercise caution and practice deliberately and sensibly. One must combine the practices with proper understanding of what they are meant to do and what they are capable and not capable of producing.

Saraha's point is that all these methods are always contrived, *chöma*[92] (Tib.) and that a non-contrived method is the best method.

Verse 23:

> *Just as Brahmins taking ghee and rice,*
> *Toss it in blazing fire expecting fair return,*
> *So those taking nectar from the essence of space,*
> *Expect the ultimate from passing experience.*

The problems that arise with these kinds of practices basically come from our attachment to the experiences produced. We crave different experiences and pleasurable experiences. If we continue to crave pleasurable experiences, we will not attain liberation. We may attain higher levels of consciousness, we may attain a certain advanced level of spiritual attainment, but still they are of the contrived variety, the tainted variety. They are still bound within the realm of karma.

This is explained with the use of the example of the Agni puja, the fire puja so dear to the Brahmans. These pujas are conducted by making burnt offerings. Various substances, particularly butter, ghee, and rice are thrown into a fire-pit. In the Vajrayana and Tantrayana we also do fire puja, known as *jinsek*[93] in Tibetan, in a similar way.

Brahmans perform these pujas thinking that by making burnt offerings they will receive spiritual rewards. Saraha assesses this as similar to tantric practice which also involves certain visualizations. For example, by visualizing a seed syllable ham to represent the very essence of *akasha*[94] (Skt.) or space, one imagines nectar-like substances flowing down so that one is filled with such nectar. With this, various ecstatic, blissful, and pleasurable sensations are experienced. Again, one can be duped by these pleasurable experiences and forget to look for *mahasukha*[95] (Skt.), the great bliss which can only come from practicing the natural path, the uncontrived path.

The main inadequacies of these various forms of tantric practice, which are very much Saraha's focus here, are that they attempt to recondition the mind. Thus, instead of trying to de-condition the mind so one can abide in one's own natural state, one is reconditioning the mind. Of course, reconditioning the mind reverses our own usual habitual mind, but to do so thinking, "This is what I have to cultivate," "I have to be good at this," "This is something I have to win over," and "I have to get rid of this, it is undesirable and something to abhor," leads one to become caught in another form of dualistic trap. We do not really find bliss this way.

As long as there is striving to get rid of something and attain something else, one cannot remain in a non-contrived way. If one's techniques or methods are contrived, one cannot be in a natural state. Without the natural state then true bliss cannot be experienced. These are the reasons these practices have the potential to distract the unwary meditator or tantric practitioner although, of course, it need not necessarily be the case.

Verse 24:

> *Using heat ascending to Brahma's abode,*
> *Stroking the uvula with the tongue—*
> *Some, attached to such congress, their mastery held dear,*
> *Call themselves yogis through pride.*

Some practitioners generate heat in the abdominal region that rises upwards and melts the life-essence in the crown region causing it to descend. By doing certain practices with the tip of the tongue rolled backwards into the back of the throat, to the uvula, they can generate great bliss. They have pleasurable experiences to which they become attached and, because of their proficiency and dexterity in doing the practices, they become conceited. Consequently they think they have obtained something very precious. They then make a big deal out of this yogic capacity, considering themselves to be yogis, but Saraha refutes that. A true yogi is not someone who can perform various yogic exercises and physical manipulations; a true yogi is one who has mastered their mind.

Again, if one becomes attached to these techniques, then one will not be free. This sort of practice then also has to be seen as limited in value.

Verse 25:

Announcing self-awareness as self-cognizing awareness
Declaring it to free what binds—
Calling a bauble an emerald because of its color,
Fools can't see what should be prized.

There are other yogis who, through meditation, may have an experience of self-awareness and then mistake this experience to be genuine self-existing, self-cognizing awareness. Due to the failure on their part to differentiate between the two, they may even give out instructions in the methods of this, claiming it will liberate others from the bondage of samsara. This is untrue. The psychic act of self-awareness on its own is not the same as self-cognizing awareness. To mistake one for the other is to mistake a cheap stone that happens to be green for a precious stone. If one is not a skillful gemologist, all gems look the same so one cannot distinguish a precious gem from a cheap imitation. Someone who does not know the difference could, in fact, purchase an imitation and treat it with great care, thinking it was the real thing.

In meditation it is very easy to mistake the simple empirical act of self-awareness for the transcendental state of self-cognizing awareness. Failure to make this distinction has led many a meditator astray. So again, one should not get too carried away by simply having an experience of self-awareness. Having had such an experience, one should not immediately announce to the world that one has attained the transcendental state of self-cognizing awareness.[96]

Verse 26:

Thinking brass is gold—
Mistaking meditative experience for realization.
Attachment to the bliss in a dream—

> *The aggregates are impermanent, how can you say*
> *such bliss is not?*

In this verse Saraha points out the differences between meditative experiences and meditative realizations.

Many a meditator has failed to make this important distinction. "Not everything that glitters is gold," as the saying goes. To mistake meditative experiences for meditative realization is like mistaking cheap yellow brass for a genuine, authentic gold nugget. And again, through various forms of tantric methods such as pranayama, one can produce many different kinds of experiences, but these experiences should not be mistaken for realization.

For example, when we go to sleep at night, we may have a very pleasant dream. Then upon awakening, because the dream was so beautiful, we may still be attached to that pleasant feeling, even though we have fully woken up and understood it was just a dream.

People who engage in these forms of practice might make claims such as, "But it is not like that, because even if the pleasures one experiences due to the meditative experiences are sullied, tainted with karmic imprints, and so forth, still, at the time of death, the consciousness becomes dislodged from the body. This consciousness will then, in its post mortem state, still be inseparable from the bliss acquired during one's lifetime." But this is false. When the body disintegrates, the pleasure associated with the meditative experiences will also disappear.

The body has to act as the medium or conduit to have any pleasurable experience. It is only because one has a body that one can engage in the various forms of yogic exercises that produce pleasurable sensations. Not having a body will necessarily mean the pleasure cannot arise. As the body itself is impermanent, so is the bliss derived from the body; the blissful experiences are contingent on the perpetuity of the body.

Verse 27:

> *The words "e" and "vam" are understood individually.*
> *By classifying four moments, four seals are set out.*
> *Some claim the experiences to be the state of union (sahaja).*
> *They are focusing on the replica in the mirror.*

E and *vam* are two words. With the E-Vam sign at our center in Melbourne[97] we put a dash between the two: E and Vam. Sometimes people have asked me why we put a dash there. It is because *e* and *vam* are two separate words and the dash is supposed to separate those two words. *E* as a Sanskrit character is triangular in shape whereas *vam* is more circular. In any case, *e* and *vam* represent the union of opposites. *E* represents wisdom and *vam* represents skillful means or compassion.

Alternatively, it represents bliss and emptiness. There are many different explanations for e-vam. A higher level explanation of e-vam is that e represents the unconditional or natural state, which is pure right from beginning, and vam represents unceasing phenomenal appearances.

Another explanation is that e represents *drenmé* (Tib.), a term that has been translated as non-memory or non-recollection or even non-mindfulness.[98] The Sanskrit *vam* is then translated as memory, recollection, or mindfulness, *drenpa*[99] (Tib.), and the letters e-vam are an explanation of that.

We then have the four moments[100] and the four seals.[101] We have to understand these four seals or four mudras (Skt.). They correspond to the four different types of bliss that are talked about in the tantric system. The four mudras are also mentioned in the Mahanuttarayoga tantra system. The first seal is *karmamudra*[102] (Skt.), and karmamudra corresponds to the experience of bliss.[103] The second mudra or seal is called *dharmamudra*[104] (Skt.), which represents great bliss.[105] The third, *samayamudra*[106] (Skt.), corresponds to transcendental bliss.[107] Then the fourth mudra is called *mahamudra*[108] (Skt.), and corresponds to co-emergent bliss.[109]

The point here is that the significance of the letters *e-vam* is understood through a gradual process of negotiating various levels of spiritual realization, attainment, and experience corresponding to the four levels of bliss and four seals or mudras.

The process one goes through is tied to remembrance and non-remembrance, recollection and non-recollection. These terms were mentioned earlier and are from tantric terminology. They may seem a bit obscure, but this is unavoidable. It is necessary to study tantric material to understand fully, but we will outline a preliminary explanation.

Let us explore remembrance and non-remembrance. In higher meditative states, in fact, mindfulness is not something one should still be practicing. One should not still be trying to practice non-forgetfulness which is what *drenpa* means. Instead, *drenmé*, the state of non-recollection, is what needs to take place. There is though, a complementary relationship existing between a state of non-remembrance and the state of remembrance. This is because they represent two aspects of one's being. For easier comprehension, one might call them something like relative and absolute aspects of one's being.

Next we will discuss the four types of bliss and the four different types of mudras. The two concepts of non-remembrance and remembrance have to be matched with what are called the four moments. These are also mentioned in the translation of the root verse which states, "By classifying four moments, four seals are set out."

At the first moment, different kinds of perceptual experiences are present and these perceptual experiences give rise to likes and dislikes. This state corresponds to the state of remembrance and the first level of bliss.

Then one makes the transition to the next level. At this stage, the activity of remembrance that had been occurring previously, in terms of different kinds of perceptual experiences, is seen as being absorbed into the state of non-remembrance, or dissipating into the sphere of non-remembrance. That then is seen as an indication of the maturation of the state of remembrance into the state of non-remembrance. This corresponds to the second moment, or moment of maturation, which corresponds to the second state of bliss.

That is then followed by the next level. Here, both remembrance and non-remembrance become absorbed into the state of uncreated-ness (*kyemé*) where there are no signs, no symbols, no characteristics, no attributes of any kind. This is marked by the third moment which is a state free of characteristics. At this moment, all thoughts of spiritual cultivation and abandonment of obstacles to the spiritual path are relinquished and the third form of bliss realized. Because one has attained that state of uncreated-ness, then neither remembrance nor non-remembrance makes an appearance. This state is marked by the seal of samayamudra.

That state is followed by a state where there is not even the notion of remembrance, non-remembrance, or uncreated-ness. All three have dissipated into the sphere of "beyond conception." At this point then, the fourth moment is secured. Then remembrance, non-remembrance, uncreated-ness, and the state beyond conception (*lodé*)—all of that—manifests. One concurrently experiences the fourth kind of bliss. This is marked by the attainment of Mahamudra. Nothing transcends the realm beyond conception which is encapsulated by the seal of Mahamudra.

As one can imagine, Saraha, being a great tantric practitioner, was very well-versed in Tantrism, so in this section he discusses many different kinds of tantric concepts. He is putting Mahamudra in the context of Tantrism and describing how the other mudras fit within Mahamudra and how Mahamudra fits in with the overall scheme of the tantric system of four mudras.

His point is that unless one attains the seal of Mahamudra, all the other seals will leave the meditator short of final realization. This is so even if the meditator has managed to experience the corresponding states of bliss, corresponding moments of enlightenment, and so on of the particular seals. They fail to achieve the final goal which is possible only through the realization of Mahamudra. If this cannot be done, it is akin to falling in love with an image in a mirror instead of looking at the real person, or seeing a reflection of the moon in a pond, and failing to see the moon.

So in this context also, Saraha's point is that we should not get too attached to karmamudra, dharmamudra, and samayamudra but instead focus our mind on the realization of Mahamudra, beyond conception, beyond attachment.

Verse 28:

> *Not understanding, deer rush*
> *Toward water that is a mirage.*
> *Similarly, the foolish cannot slake their parching thirst—*
> *Latching onto bliss, they claim it as the ultimate.*

Saraha is stating that when it all boils down to it, we should determine the fundamental focus of our mind when we engage in spiritual practice. Does our focus lie on what is immediate and empirically present, or does it rest on the transcendental realm? Even in terms of our practice, if we pursue our spiritual goals with our focus solely on empirical things—meaning things which are dependent on causes and conditions—then whatever positive results we gain will be transient, impermanent. These wonderful experiences will arise and dissipate, arise and dissipate, so are not really trustworthy. And if we think that through these means we are pursuing the "eternal" or transcendental center of our being, the dharmakaya, we have everything backwards.

This is like a deer rushing forward thinking there is water in the distance, only to be disappointed because what they are rushing towards is a mirage and there is no water. If, through our attempts to satisfy our thirst for spiritual nourishment, we try to drink up all the temporary comfort of the encouraging experiences we have, then we fail to establish ourselves on a secure foundation. We will not realize the eternal, unchanging foundation of our being because we will be too involved with the ever-changing permutations of our experiences. We will not be anchored to a stable center. If that is so, we will not find liberation from the cyclic existence that is samsara. In our pursuit of temporary bliss, eternal bliss will literally slip through our fingers.

That then completes Saraha's warnings against incorrect practices and his explanations of the dangers involved with non-Mahamudra types of practices—if one develops fixation on them. From Saraha's perspective, in the end they will leave us wanting. While these practices may act as supplements, we need to see Mahamudra as our main practice and also main goal.

PART 6

Explaining the Mahamudra Method

The following verses then explain the Mahamudra method. Four different instructions are given in relation to this section of the practice.

Verse 29:

> *The truth of experienced reality corresponds to non-remembrance—*
> *Remembrance of mind that is perceptual experience dissipates into this.*
> *The state that is revealed as, then the supreme of supreme—*
> *The genuine supreme. Friends, you should know these.*

We have discussed remembrance, non-remembrance, the uncreated state, and the state beyond conception[110] already, in relation to the four mudras. We will go through these again in order to understand Mahamudra in relation to remembrance, non-remembrance, the state of uncreated-ness, and the state beyond conception.

First, Saraha says we have to exercise remembrance or memory, mindfulness—all of them—as part of our meditation. How do we do that? We do it by focusing on the empirical, by focusing on what we experience, and by determining that nothing we experience has objective existence independent of the mind. We have to determine that through recollection, remembrance, and mindfulness. That should lead to the state of non-remembrance; one should not remain satisfied with that initial level. If one realizes that mindfulness is the same as mind, then one will realize mindfulness/remembrance/recollection are not something separate from mind. That will then cease to be something that mind does. There is no separation between the mind and remembrance and this then leads to the realization of non-remembrance.

Once one has realized that non-separation between remembrance and mind, and realized the state of non-remembrance, that state then will be revealed as uncreated. It is not produced by causes and conditions. One thus attains the uncreated state. While the state of non-remembrance is already an exalted state, there is a state that follows from that. This state of uncreatedness is called the supreme.

Again, while already being an exalted state, the supreme state is followed by the ultimate state, which is the state beyond conception. That is why this state, the state beyond conception, is called the supreme of the supreme, *chogi chok*[111] in Tibetan. This state beyond conception, the supreme of supreme, is equated with Buddhahood. These are called the four symbolic instructions, *da shi*[112] in Tibetan. As the root verse states: "...the supreme of supreme—the genuine supreme. Friends, you should know these"—these four. There are alternative ways of matching the four sets of fours, but we do not need to discuss those.

Verse 30:

> *Non-remembrance corresponds to a samadhi.*
> *Completely untainted by the afflictions,*
> *Like a swamp-grown utpala unaffected by mud,*
> *Neither samsara's faults nor enlightened qualities obscure it.*

There are also four different kinds of samadhi, which have to be matched with the other states mentioned in the previous verses.

There is a samadhi, elegantly expressed in Tibetan, which means something like "lion-like samadhi".[113] This samadhi conveys non-remembrance/non-recollection/non-mindfulness, as represented by the utpala flower which is in no way dirtied by the mud in which it grows. This is revealed through the state of non-wavering. The state of remembrance, the first of the states Saraha presents, corresponds to what is called "illusion-like samadhi."[114] The state of the uncreated corresponds to the "heroic samadhi"[115] which enables one to go beyond things empirical. The state beyond conception corresponds to the "vajra-like samadhi",[116] the highest level of samadhi one can attain, which reveals the nature of all things while not conflating their differences, and this is revealed through Mahamudra.

Verse 31:

Having certainty all things are illusion-like,
Take the moment that is transcendence, and rest with it.
In minds with this revealed, ignorance is brought to a halt.
Self-arisen and beyond conceptualization, the nature of
mind is abiding.

This verse explains that at the level of mindfulness/recollection/remembrance, there is the experience of phenomena in their myriad forms. These appearances will occur because they are dependent upon causes and conditions. Their nature, however, is unwavering and not dependent on causes and conditions. Therefore, unlike the things themselves, the nature of things is abiding so the concepts of coming into being and ceasing to exist do not apply. In terms of the reality of things, unlike the things themselves it does not come into being, does not dwell anywhere, and does not go out of existence.

Because of that, there is complete union between the empirical phenomenal appearance of things and the nature of these things. There is no conflict between the two; they are not adversarial, their relationship is one of harmony. So therefore, while the phenomena appear the way they do, their nature always remains empty.

The meditator's experience of this is revealed through the non-divisibility of bliss and emptiness, the non-divisibility of awareness and emptiness, and the non-divisibility of clarity and emptiness. It is revealed through this series of unitive experiences: bliss and emptiness, awareness and emptiness, clarity and emptiness, and so on. Even though, conceptually, we can distinguish all of these as being separate, in themselves bliss and emptiness, clarity and emptiness, emptiness and awareness, and so on, are also not separate. Their nature is also abiding reality, the same as everything else. Through that, one realizes non-remembrance.

Although these appearances themselves are the product of causes and conditions and they appear—and this includes even things within the mind, so whatever appears to the mind—in their nature they are not caused. When one realizes that then one sees, one attains, the level of uncreated-ness. This is why it is said the nature of mind has never been caused to come into existence and for this reason it is abiding.

Verse 32:

Appearance, from the outset, is clarity, not-caused in nature.
Let phenomena, either visible or without form, be.
Rest continuously in the nature of the mind—the only
concentration.
Flawless non-mentation[117] *is not absorption.*

What do meditators need to do if, while meditating, discursive thoughts come up or if they experience phenomena? This may occur even though, a moment earlier, they may have been in a state of non-remembrance. If one has been roused from that state of non-remembrance, with the mind stirred up yet again seeing various images of different colored objects and so forth, one need not be alarmed. Whatever has arisen in that state of arousal will dissipate back into the state of non-remembrance.

Verse 33:

Intellect, mind, and what appears to it are one's natural state.
Our experiences of the world or otherwise are one's natural state.
Everything perceived or doing the perceiving is one's natural state.
Even lust, anger, ignorance, and enlightened mind are one's
natural state.

It doesn't matter whether one is experiencing something totally mundane in quality, texture, and substance or something exalted, a more rarefied state of consciousness—in either case, one needs to realize that nothing that one experiences can occur independently of one's natural state of being. In that sense, everything one experiences is permeated by Mahamudra.

In order to attain the state beyond conception which is Mahamudra, one has to realize that nothing we experience can be outside the Mahamudra state. So when we see something, then that object, the subject who perceives that object—everything involved with that perceptual experience—is in fact not separate from the state beyond conception. The state beyond conception reveals itself through these myriad ways, through the variegated experiences. If one has the real Mahamudra perspective, then all the causes of samsaric bondage, such as lust, anger, ignorance, and so forth that we think we need to renounce, as well as the bodhichitta[118] (Skt.) and insight into emptiness that we think we need to cultivate, should be seen as permeated by this state beyond conception. In meditation one should not allow the mind go into a state of focusing on a meditational object.

Verse 34:

A lamp is lit against the darkness of ignorance.
The discriminating intellect shows what's there.
So mind's obscurations are discarded.
Focus on natural non-clinging.

Here, Saraha discusses how to practice this in relation to listening, reflecting, and meditating. First, he mentions the need to practice mindfulness. At the beginning we need to carry the lamp. Mindfulness is like a small lamp that we have but, because we are groveling in the dark, even if we try to think about emptiness, we are only conceptualizing about it so we are none the wiser for it. That state is still ignorant and thinking and conceptualizing about it will not shed any light on it and lift our ignorance. Therefore, we will not realize our own mind from doing this. What then will lift that ignorance? Reading about emptiness, conceptualizing about emptiness, and contemplating on emptiness will help but if one does not meditate, one will still remain in the dark. One needs to bring in some light and to do that we need to carry the torch of mindfulness.

Again, we have to be very careful about this notion and appreciate this is simply a convenient device we need to resort to. The mindfulness we are exercising is one of mere non-forgetfulness, mere remembrance. This mere remembrance has to be employed in order to illuminate the darkness that pervades our mind so that the five kinds of wisdom inherent in the nature of mind itself can be ignited by this torch. How do we use that torch to ignite the five wisdoms: wisdom of accomplishment; wisdom of equanimity; wisdom of discrimination; mirror-like wisdom; and wisdom of suchness? For that we need specific instructions from a meditation master. Relying on these instructions, we should then use the other torch, the torch of listening to the teachings, and contemplation on the teachings.

That will also bring intellectual, conceptual illumination.

In this case, one should do study and reflection as needed. One should not study and reflect on these things just for the sake of study and reflection but in order to aid one's meditational practice. One's meditational practice should be the focus, not the study and reflection. If study and reflection are not put into the service of one's meditational development, then, again, one has failed to carry the torch of intellectual illumination properly and use it correctly. Ultimately, all of these should aid one to have genuine and unadulterated meditation.

Verse 35:

> *Neither negating nor establishing,*
> *Non-fixation is inconceivable.*
> *The discriminating intellect binds the foolish.*
> *Inseparability, co-emergence, is utter purity.*

The above verse concerns how to meditate. What should we do in Mahamudra meditation? What we need to do, in essence, with Mahamudra meditation is develop proper understanding. That proper understanding has to be such that it comes from inner conviction and is not simply because we are well-versed in the dialectical methods used by various schools of Buddhist thought. It should not have to do with propositional statements, either in defense of a particular philosophical position or used as an aid to demolish someone else's point of view. In other words, conviction should not simply be based on the establishment of a certain philosophical view; it has to be based on one's own experience of spiritual development.

Meditation also has to be free of the concept of meditating, as if meditation is something that one has to "do." Saraha asserts that if we really learn to use mindfulness properly, then we will realize that we do not need to establish or negate anything.

The point is really about entering into one's natural state rather than establishing a point of view about it. If we apply mindfulness in the correct manner, then the state of non-mindfulness or the state of non-remembrance will naturally occur. In other words, one does not need to hanker after the accumulation of any positive qualities and attributes either.

Verse 36:

Not through the reasoning of one and many alone,
But by simply recognizing, are migrators liberated.
Recognizing the apparent, remain in meditation—
The non-wavering state. Enter into that.

The reasoning of one and many is the Madhyamaka reasoning, as well as the form of reasoning used by Buddhist logicians such as Dignaga and Chandrakirti. They try to arrive at emptiness through the use of reasoning but, in the end, reasoning alone will not lead to the actual realization of the unsullied state. The unsullied state will only be realized through meditation, but in such a way that conflicting emotions and so forth are not seen as something that must be renounced or discarded. Instead, it is realized through accessing one's own natural state of being. As one enters into one's own natural state, mindfulness or remembrance, recollection, turns into non-remembrance; non-remembrance turns into the non-remembrance of emptiness; non-remembrance turns into the state of uncreated-ness; and uncreated-ness turns into the state beyond conception.

So in meditation one does not need to worry about what is to be avoided or what is to be cultivated. What the meditator needs to do is simply be aware of the tendency to become drowsy, to fall under the influence of stupor, on one hand, and mental agitation, on the other. If one just remains in that state, then one will be in that state of non-wavering. Remaining in that unwavering state is meditation.

PART 7

Result

Verse 37:

> *Attaining the place of all-pervading bliss,*
> *The mind that sees is actualized.*
> *As for being a place to which one has gone—*
> *It is not something separate.*

From the practice of Mahamudra, unlike the other practices mentioned, the bliss attained would be the co-emergent bliss—unadulterated, unchanging bliss. This bliss is all-pervading because one is in a state of total non-fabrication and one has actualized buddha's authentic state of being. Even though we may talk about approaching enlightenment, travelling towards enlightenment, embarking on the path to enlightenment, and so on, as if enlightenment is a place that we arrive at, in actuality there is no separate place that we travel to when we attain enlightenment. Enlightenment is attained in the present. It is only the mind that makes that separation.

Verse 38:

> *The seed of blissful joy*
> *Arisen as petals of the sublime state—*
> *There is no outflow to the ten directions then,*
> *Just the fruition of blissful lack of conceptual elaboration.*

The co-emergent bliss that one attains as a result of Mahamudra practice is not only untainted by the elements of samsara but it is even free of nirvanic constraints. It is thus totally free of all constraints. This state is pure right from beginning, so therefore nirvana has nothing to add to it to make it any better. One realizes the body of bliss at the time of fruition. All three aspects of buddha's being: the physical aspect, the communicative aspect, and the authentic state become manifest and actualized. They are not three separate things joined to form one, but they are one, in the authentic state of buddha's being. The other two, the physical and communicative aspects, are inseparable from the authentic state of buddha's being.

The authentic state permeates all aspects of the totality of one's being. But having attained one's goal, having arrived at the state of enlightenment, then one does not cease to operate. On the contrary, the buddha activity continues through the realization of the physical and communicative aspects of buddha's being so that as long as there is a need for a buddha to appear then, one would appear for others' benefit.

Verse 39:

> *Without absolute existence in terms of "by whom,"*
> *"where" and "to whom,"*
> *Benefitting wherever and whoever as needed—*
> *Appearing as having form, caring without attachment,*
> *Yet empty in nature.*

The nirmanakaya or physical aspect of buddha's being appears. One would appear everywhere one was needed and continue to work for the benefit of others. How one benefits others, again, does not waver from the confluence of relative truth and absolute truth. Beneficial acts are performed in the world and beings do genuinely receive benefit but at the same time, from the ultimate point of view, the buddhas and the sentient creatures in need of aid or help are not separate. Even the way in which buddhas appear works with the same principle as everything else. That is, buddhas do appear but the nature of buddhas does not waver from ultimate reality which is emptiness.

Verse 40:

> *"Like a pig I wallow in the samsaric mire,"*
> *Yet with a flawless mind, where's the fault?*
> *Unaffected by anything,*
> *How is it I am bound?*

At the end, Saraha stops singing to the king. At this point, the king makes a tongue-in-cheek comment to Saraha: "Saraha, I have heard what you have had to say about spiritual practices. Well, what you are saying is that pigs have got it right! Pigs do not cultivate anything and they do not denounce anything; they are quite happy to play in the mud." This is *langdor gang-yang mepa*[119] in Tibetan. *Lang* means "to cultivate," *dor*, "to renounce," and *gang-yang mepa* means "nothing."

The basic point of this verse is that first there is the tongue-in-cheek exchange described then the verse concludes with a comment on the progression involved for the practitioner. This progression is similar to that portrayed in the ox-herding pictures found in the Zen tradition. First the ox-herder has to tame or get to know the ox, then they become friends, then finally the ox allows the herder to ride him. At the end there is no ox and there is no rider—he then returns to appear in the market place.

A similar thing occurs after attaining enlightenment in that one re-enters samsara for the benefit of others. But when one re-enters samsara, one is not touched one iota by the "filth" of the samsaric condition. One re-enters and benefits all sentient beings, being in the world completely yet not touched by the world. A buddha is thus in the world, but not of the world. Nothing going on in the world impacts on the buddha's attainment, so there is no possibility of relapse or sliding back, of slowly getting corrupted by the world.

This completes the preliminary, main, and concluding sections of this doha.

Traleg Kyabgon Rinpoche's Concluding Remarks

I hope you have received some benefit from going over this doha. I also hope you will deepen your understanding of the Mahamudra tradition and practice and perhaps read more about Saraha and get to know his dohas a little more intimately, particularly if you are following the Kagyü tradition. As mentioned, Saraha holds a very special place in our lineage. We trace our lineage back to him and he has influenced subsequent generations of leaders of the lineage.

I personally feel that not too many people coming to Tibetan Buddhism actually want to engage in all the tantric rituals involved in the tradition, even though they like the teachings and want to follow them. A simpler, more easily done meditation is then very useful and very beneficial. On the one hand, Mahamudra is advanced because it is what we have to realize but, on the other, as a practice, it is not so advanced that we cannot take it on. To reiterate a point made at the very beginning of this book, if you read the Mahamudra manuals, you will find they explain everything step by step, as if the reader has no knowledge at all. It is thus not out of bounds. Mahamudra is very important in our lineage, and it seems fitting to encourage it.

Notes

1. *do ha mdzod ces bya ba spyod pa'i glu* More than one version of the Tibetan text for the root verses exists, presenting issues for translation. The translation of the root verses by this editor was thus not based on a single text version. See Bibliography for Tibetan root texts, Tibetan commentaries, and English translations of the root verses and commentary consulted.

2. Karma 'phrin las pa (456-539), a Kagyu scholar who was also the teacher of the Eight Karmapa.

3. *do ha skor gsum gyi tshig don gyi rnam bshad sems kyi rnam thar gsal ba bston pa'i me long* The version of the Tibetan text for this commentary as used by Traleg Rinpoche is unknown.

4. Herbert Guenther, *The Royal Song of Saraha: A Study in the History of Buddhist Thought* (Seattle: University of Washington Press.1969, Reprint: Shambhala, 1973)

5. Skye med bde chen

6. A detailed explanation of the Four Yogas of Mahamudra can be found in Traleg Kyabgon, *Moonbeams of Mahamudra: The Classic Meditation Manual* (Carlton North, Victoria: Shogam Publications, 2015), pp. 349-341.

7. *brda*

8. *dran pa, dran med, skye med, and blo 'das*

9. *mahāmudrā*

10. *mahāsiddha Mahā* denotes "great" and siddha denotes "saint" or "adept." There are usually eighty-four *mahāsiddhas* listed, although eighty-four may be a number arrived at simply for convenience.

11. *śamatha* Commonly referred to in English as tranquility meditation.

12. *rdzogs chen*

13. *śūnya*

14. *śūnyatā*

15. *rang grol*

16. *grol lam*

17. *thab lam*

18. *Nāropa* (c.a. 1016-1110) was an Indian tantric mahasiddha considered an important figure in the Kagyü tradition. The *naro chödruk* (n'a ro chos drug)(Tib.) are also sometimes referred to as Naropa's six yogas or six doctrines.

19. *vipaśyanā* Commonly referred to in English as insight meditation.

20. This is most likely a reference to the Tibetan term *tha mal gyi shes pa*.

21. *Abhidharma* refers to the systematized set of Buddhist teachings that could be described as dealing with Buddhist psychology.

22. *bcos pa*

23. *bcos pa'i sgom*

24. *ngo bo gcig la ldog pa tha de*

25. *sahaja*

26. *mnyam pa nyid*

27. *dharmakāya*

28. The Mahamudra lineage supplication known in Tibetan as *Dorjé Chang Thungm*a.

29. *rnam rtog ngo bo chos skur gsungs pa bzhin*
30. *'khrul pa*
31. *zung 'jug*
32. *rtsal*
33. *nu pa* Often glossed as "capacity" or "power."
34. This text is known in brief in Tibetan as *phyag chen nges don rgya mtsho*. Traleg Rinpoche's oral commentary on the text has been published as *The Ninth Karmapa, Wangchuk Dorje's Ocean of Certainty* (New York: KTD Publications, 2011).
35. *yāna*
36. *spang blang re dogs dang bral ba*
37. *gnas 'gyu rig gsum*
38. *gnas cha and gsal cha*
39. *ci yang ma yin cir yang 'char ba la*
40. *lhun grub*
41. *ma bdag pa'i snang ba*
42. *bdag pa'i snang ba, bdag snang*
43. *ci yang ma yin cir yang 'char ba la/ ma 'gags rol par 'char ba'i sgom chen la/ 'khor 'das dbyer med rtogs par byin gyis rlobs/*
44. *rol pa*
45. *rol pa 'char ba*
46. *bde chen*
47. *bde chen rgyun chad med*
48. *vikalpa*
49. *rnam rtog*
50. *prapañca*

51. *spros pa*

52. *nyon mongs lam khyer*

53. Rangjung Dorjé, *Song of Karmapa: The Aspiration of the Mahamudra of True Meaning*, verse 13: *'di nyid ma rtogs 'khor ba'i rgya mtshor 'khor/ 'di nyid rtogs na sangs rgyas gzhan na med/*

54. *āyatana*

55. *skandha*

56. *nyams*

57. *rtogs pa*

58. *'od gsal*

59. The Tibetan term for meditation here is *nyam shak* (mnyam bzhag) and for post-meditation is *jé thop* (rjes thob).

60. The term *dohā* is used to refer to a mystical inspirational song. Traditionally, these are not composed, but spontaneously extemporized, the words then recalled by students.

61. These have been translated into English by Herbert Guenther in *Ecstatic Spontaneity: Saraha's three cycles of dohā* (Berkeley: Asian Humanities Press, 1993).

62. *Dohākośa nāma caryāgīti*

63. *do ha mdzod ces bya ba spyod pa'i glu*

64. The line that precedes this in some versions of the root text, "I prostrate to Noble Mañjuśrī," was not mentioned by Traleg Rinpoche, most likely on the grounds that it is Karma Trinlépa's supplication for his commentary.

65. The choice of the English words "high waves" and "rollers" used by Traleg Rinpoche here was based on the rendition of *ba* (rba) and *lap* (rlabs) as "waves and rollers" by Herbert

Guenther in *The Royal Song of Saraha* (Berkeley: Shambhala Publications, 1973), pp. 63: *As calm water lashed by wind/ Turns into waves and rollers/ So the king thinks of Saraha/ In many ways, although one man.* The two syllables of the Tibetan word *balap* are commonly translated together as "waves."

66. *kye ma*

67. *dpe don*

68. *sahajajñāna*

69. *lhan cig skyes pa'i ye shes*

70. *mahākarunā, snying rje chen po*

71. *stong nyid snying rje'i snying po can*

72. *ro gcig*

73. *nirmānakāya*

74. *sambhogakāya*

75. *dharmakāya*

76. *samādhi*

77. *dag pa gnyis ldan*

78. *rgyud bla ma, Mahāyāna Uttaratantra*

79. *rang bzhin rnam dag*

80. *glo bur bral dag*

81. *dpe*

82. *gcig du bral gyi gtan tshigs*

83. *dpyad sgom*

84. *'jog sgom*

85. *lam phyag rgya chen po*

86. *karmamudrā*

87. *las kyi phyag rgya*

88. *kāmarūpa*

89. *prāṇāyāma*

90. *prāṇa, nāḍi, and bindu*

91. *abhiṣekha*

92. *bcos ma*

93. *sbyin sreg*

94. *ākāśa*

95. *mahāsukha*

96. In the original talks, rather than consistently using "an experience of self-awareness" versus "the transcendental state of self-cognizing awareness," Traleg Rinpoche used a variety of terms. Specifically, for the term used here, "an experience of self-awareness," he did in one instance use "an experience of self-cognizing awareness." Self-cognizing awareness was contracted to self-awareness to avoid confusion. Thrangu Rinpoche, when discussing verse 25 in *A Song for the King: Saraha on Mahamudra Meditation*, (Boston: Wisdom Publications, 2006), pp. 86-89, provides a detailed explanation of the terms involved.

97. Refers to E-Vam Institute, Melbourne, Australia.

98. This term, pronounced "drenmé" with a retroflexed "r" (dran med) appears in verse 29 and is discussed further there. The following is an excerpt from an unpublished series of talks given by Traleg Rinpoche on the Mahamudra View in 2005: *Mahamudra places a great emphasis on trying to remain in the natural way. If we can remain in the natural way, the full force of wisdom-consciousness will gradually begin to take effect. If*

we cannot remain in the natural way, if we are too deliberative in our practice, we will just reinforce our old habit patterns. This is why the concept of mindlessness (rather than mindfulness) is sometimes mentioned. In Saraha's Dohas, Herbert Guenther translates this term as "non-memory." Mindlessness means that remaining with luminosity is not something that we need to do with deliberateness. The mind does not intentionally focus on anything or seize onto anything. Intentionally seizing onto something is probably what is meant by vikalpa (Skt.) or namtok (rnam rtog) (Tib.), a term that is usually translated as "giving rise to conceptual proliferation." Also see Appendix 4 of *A Song for the King* for Michele Martin's helpful discussion of this term.

99. *dran pa*
100. *kechikma* (skad cig ma) in Tibetan
101. *chagya* (phyag rgya) in Tibetan
102. *karmamudrā, legya* (las rgya) in Tibetan
103. *gawa* (dga' ba) in Tibetan
104. *dharmamudrā, chögya* (chos rgya) in Tibetan
105. *choga* (mchog dga') in Tibetan
106. *samayamudrā, damgya* (dam rgya) in Tibetan
107. *gadral,* (dga' bral) in Tibetan
108. *mahāmudrā, chakchen* (phyag chen) in Tibetan
109. *lhenchik kyega* (lhan cig skyes dga') in Tibetan
110. In Tibetan, these terms are *drenpa, drenmé, kyemé,* and *lodé* (dran pa, dran med, skye med, and blo 'das).
111. *mchog gi mchog*
112. *brda bzhi*

113. *sengé nampar tsewai tingé dzin* (sengge rnam par rtse ba'i ting nge 'dzin) in Tibetan

114. *gyuma tabui tingé dzin* (sgyu ma lta bu'i ting nge 'dzin) in Tibetan

115. *pawar drowai tingé dzin* (dpa' bar 'gro ba'i ting nge 'dzin) in Tibetan

116. *dorjé tabui tingé dzin* (rdo rje lta bu'i ting nge 'dzin) in Tibetan

117. The term "non-mentation" found in the fourth line of the verse is yila mijepa (yid la mi byed pa)(Tib.), *amanisākāra* (Skt.).

118. *bodhicitta*

119. *blang dor gang yang med pa*

Bibliography

Tibetan Works

Karma 'phrin las pa. *Do ha skor gsum gyi tshig don gyi rnam bshad sems kyi rnam thar gsal ba bston pa'i me long.* Sarnath: Vajravidhya Institute Library, 2009. The Tibetan Buddhist Resource Centre holds digitally scanned images of this text. See www.tbrc.org and number W1KG4306.

—— *Rgyal po do ha'i ti ka 'bring po sems kyi rnam thar ston pa'i me long. In Do ha skor gsum gyi ti ka 'bring po.* 165-222 (roman 159-216). Thimphu, Bhutan: Druk Sherig Press, 1984. The Tibetan Buddhist Resource Centre holds digitally scanned images of this text. See www.tbrc.org and number W10426.

Saraha. *Do ha mdzod gyi glu.* The Degé edition of this text can be located at www.adarsha.dharma-treasure.org. See ADARSHA: degetengyur sutra ID - DT1162, volume {zhi} (52) page {zhi} 52-1-26b6~52-1-28b6)

English Language works

Dowman, Keith. *Saraha's Royal Song.* http://keithdowman.net/mahamudra/sarahas-royal-song.html.

Guenther, Herbert V. 1969. *The Royal Song of Saraha: A Study in the History of Buddhist Thought.* Seattle: University of Washington Press. Reprint: Shambhala, 1973.

—— 1993. *Ecstatic Spontaneity: Saraha's Three Cycles of Dohā.* Berkeley, CA: Asian Humanities Press.

Kyabgon, Traleg. 2011. *The Ninth Karmapa, Wangchuk Dorje's Ocean Of Certainty.* New York: KTD Publications.

Kyabgon, Traleg. 2015. *Moonbeams of Mahamudra: The Classic Meditation Manual.* Carlton North, Victoria: Shogam Publications.

Jackson, Roger. 1994. *"Guenther's Saraha: A detailed review of Ecstatic Spontaneity." Journal of the International Association of Buddhist Studies* 17.1: 111-143.

Namgyal, Dakpo Tashi. Kunzang, Erik Pema, tr. 2001 *Clarifying the Natural State.* Boudanath: Rangjung Yeshe Publications.

Thrangu Rinpoche, Kenchen. Martin, Michele, ed. 2006. *A Song for the King: Saraha on Mahamudra Meditation.* Boston: Wisdom Publications.

Schaeffer, Kurtis R. 2005. *Dreaming the Great Brahmin: Tibetan Traditions of the Buddhist Poet-Saint Saraha.* Oxford: Oxford University Press.

Wangchuk Dorjé, the Ninth Gyalwang Karmapa. 2001. *Mahamudra: The Ocean of definitive Meaning.* Translated by Elizabeth M. Callahan. Seattle: Nithartha International.

Index